the
# Oak Tree
# Source

## How to Become a Man of Strength, Substance, and Spirituality

**Britt Gusmus**

**The Oak Tree Source**
How to Become a Man of Strength, Substance, and Spirituality
© 2022 by Britt Gusmus. All rights reserved.

Book Consultant: Judith Briles, The Book Shepherd
Editors: Judith Briles and Margaret Ireland
Cover, Interior Design, and eBook conversion:
Rebecca Finkel, F+P Graphic Design

Books may be purchased in quantity
by contacting the publisher directly at
IsaColt Publishing
(720) 297-8067  |  Britt@BrittGusmus.com

Library of Congress Control Number: data on file
Hardcover: 979-8-9857487-1-0
Paperback: 979-8-9857487-2-7
eBook: 979-8-9857487-0-3
Audiobook: 979-8-9857487-3-4
Ingram Spark: 979-8-9857487-4-1

Christian Living  |  Personal Growth  |  Leadership  |  Men

First Edition
Printed in the USA

*This book is dedicated to my family.*

*Carrie, Isabel, and Colton.*

*I dedicate my life to being a source of strength*

*and substance for the three of you.*

*I am continually amazed at what*

*God has created with us and in us.*

*May we continue to grow strong and sturdy together*

*and as the individuals God created each one of us to be.*

# Contents

# Author's Note

As you read this book, my prayer is that wherever you are in your journey, man or woman, you find hope and inspiration. Through this story you see what it takes to overcome the demons that hold you back from the life you were meant to live. Manhood is so much more than Western culture has portrayed it to be. Being the "head" of anything, an organization, a team, a household, starts by being its foundation, its source. The source can be a thankless, sacrificial, often criticized, and in no way glamorous position. Much like the position Jesus Christ occupied during his time in leadership on earth. What could possibly be the benefit of this type of leadership? If you decide to lead like Jesus does, the benefits become growth of immovable roots of strength, mentally, emotionally, spiritually, roots of respect and honor among your family, friends, and colleagues. Most importantly, you will develop a relationship with the God of the Universe that enhances and expands your presence like the power and reach of an oak tree. While reading this book, focus on the principles of self-discovery, integrating your thoughts, emotions, behaviors, and actions so that you can experience a wholeness of mind, spirit, and body that is powerful, that creates a purposeful satisfaction that overflows with life-giving qualities.

The message of *The Oak Tree Source* is what I believe to be divinely inspired to bring forth a way of living for men that creates meaning and significance that answers questions about who you are, who you were made to be, and how you go about becoming that. If you practice the principles in this book, your life will change, your passion will be ignited, and you will understand what it means to be led. The ability to humble yourself and be led by a loving God who is greater than you is the ultimate act of leadership.

Go deep!

—BRITT

# Foreword

Britt has painstakingly taken all the lessons from his life, both good and bad, to give us a deep insight into the mind and soul of young boys. These same boys will carry all they learned or didn't learn through this life. They are our sons, our husbands, our fathers, our grandsons, our nephews, our neighbors.

What a beautiful unveiling of the human soul and the longing that resides within each of us. Ever the scholar, Britt draws from the bible, Brene Brown and others in literature to further strengthen his missives. What a joy this book is. My hope? That you will gather round the dinner table and discuss it together. For when we come together we can become collective oak trees, glorious in stature and able to provide emotional nourishment and shelter for so many lives.

Get your notebook or journal and prepare to go on the journey of a lifetime. You will be forever changed.

—RACHEL JOY BARIBEAU  
Former National Sportscaster  
Founder of *www.ImChangingtheNarrative.org*

# 1 Awakenings

Enter through the narrow gate. For wide is the gate and broad is the road that leads to destruction, and many enter through it.

Matthew 7:13

# chapter one

# The Source

*I yearned for kinship, belonging, and connection.*

The roles of peacekeeper and caregiver aren't ones associated with developing young boys. Rarely can they cope with or set emotional boundaries, leaving one option for an outlet of their bubbling emotions: sports. Sports were a tremendous refuge for me. Sports became the starting point (source) for my survival. Survival meant identity, value, love, kinship, and connection. I found those by playing on a team. The natural collaboration that happens on a team promotes purity. There was pursuit of one common goal, which strengthened the bond of all the people involved. With that bond came jealousy, bitterness, division, and hurt.

The purity of having a source to connect with and common purpose to ascribe to became muddled by the wants and needs of individuals. However, along with sports came authoritarian figures with good intentions, but finding balance between tough love and authentic encouragement never found its way to my heart.

I played soccer because I wanted to belong. I was accused of not hustling enough. I played baseball because I wanted to belong. I was told I needed to be a pitcher. And the first time I pitched in a park full of people all watching me, I was the loneliest I'd ever felt. Then the feeling of freedom—real freedom—came over me when I strapped on a football helmet for the first time.

In the act of spiking the football after scoring my first touchdown, bitterness, jealousy, and hurt were as far away as they could be. And I spiked that ball with all of my might. The satisfaction I felt that moment opened the door to what would become my purpose. Not only was that spike of the football a release from bitterness and disappointment, it was also a purposefully satisfying act that guided me back to purity, and the source of everything *kephalē*, the art of leading and leadership.

As a starting point (source) for others, we are called to endure the Refiner's Fire so that our life has substance. Substance is the stuff we are made of—the most important or essential part of something, the essential meaning of something. When a mineral is stripped down to its essential parts, this is where it has its most value. Just like the mineral, we need to be stripped of bitterness, jealousy, and anger so that we can become a source of substance and strength, which leads to purposeful satisfaction.

In a world filled with pride, arrogance, and self-centeredness, I had many hard lessons to learn. Lessons that continue every day. When a mirror is put in front of you that reflects love, purity, honesty, strength, and compassion, you have two choices:

1. You can turn and run.

2. You can walk toward that light every day, one step at a time.

I was shown the mirror every day I walked into a meeting of Alcoholics Anonymous.

**I knew I did not want to go back to the prison of shame.**

Early on, the grip of shame generated from my parents' divorce. Surely I must have been the cause. Maybe I was not performing as well as others felt I should or could. Maybe I could never perform well enough to be loved. I carried around the feeling that I was never "enough" for anyone ... including myself. And this feeling was reinforced when I finally admitted to having a problem. My internal dialogue surfaced in a room full of recovering alcoholics and users, reminding me I wasn't good enough. I was a loser.

This negativity prevented me from embracing the benefits of looking in this mirror of amazing wounded healers that were available to me. I kept coming back though, walking through those doors, looking for a source that could spread seeds of hope, joy, and purposeful satisfaction.

I knew I did not want to go back to the prison of shame.

*Men walk this tightrope where any sign of weakness elicits shame, and so they're afraid to make themselves vulnerable for fear of looking weak.*

—Brené Brown, *Dare to Lead*

# coach gus' insights

When you swallow truth about yourself and let that truth bring about change and growth, it makes you stronger—not weaker.

# chapter two

# The Oak Tree

*Enveloped with a sense of protection,*
*I felt like I had tannin from a massive tree's bark*
*protecting me and creating purity within me.*

A huge oak can deliver 10,000 acorns or more in one
year providing nourishment and shelter for a myriad of
life. Every season, animals ranging from elk and rabbits to
crows and squirrels depend on the fruit of the great oak.
In its breadth and width, it provides shelter from the sun
and rain, a glorious place for birds to roost and nest.

The acorn is such a vital piece of nourishment for some
species that they alter their habitat and living patterns in
response to the volume of acorn production. The oak tree is a
source of strength, substance, and service to all that encounter it.

The oak comes in many different sizes and widths but its
trunk—the substance of the tree—is strong. This strength and
enduring quality of the oak tree is aided by the natural compound
"tannin" that helps protect the tree bark from fungi and other
insects that could damage the tree. Even more peculiar is that

tannin helps leaves and flowers radiate beauty, especially leaves in their final stages of change during the autumn season.

For a source to sustain its environment and provide strength and substance, it first must have the character and substance to be that source. If you think about the oak tree from the perspective of a provider, and it comes into full maturity over a lengthy period of time, it is astonishing how many living organisms the tree can affect.

**"If you don't stand for something, you will fall for anything."**

Question: What if you changed your movement patterns based on the essentials to survive? It seems most people go to great lengths to provide comfort for themselves with material goods and monetary security. Another question: What if the source of your strength is rooted in eternal inspiration that satisfies your instincts and human desire? Could your movement patterns be endless? Could mine?

The Black Activist Malcolm X said, "If you don't stand for something, you will fall for anything." This is true of the principles and values that guide you. Even when conditions change, if you know what *source* is and trust that it will give you the nourishment you need no matter the season or pattern, you will grow strong and sturdy like an oak tree. As your roots grow stronger and deeper in the source of all life, your life becomes filled with substance, purity, and rich significance like the tannin of an oak tree.

A life of significance and substance leads to a set of morals, which leads to building a character that influences others in a positive way. Significance and substance are the building blocks for transformational leadership.

Enveloped with a sense of protection, I felt like I had tannin from a massive tree's bark protecting me and creating purity within me.

Seen from the symbolic perspective, the oak tree is a symbol of nobility, honor, and authority. These principles were practiced and exemplified in such amazing measure through Jesus Christ. Jesus is the source of all life. The Greek word *kephalē* used in two of the Apostle Paul's letters to explain the relationship between husbands and wives and has traditionally been interpreted as the husband is the "head" or "leader" of the wife and household.

**The source and sustainer of and for my life was far from stable.**

Western culture has lived this interpretation for centuries. In the United States it has played out in colonial America in the lack of individual rights for women. A practice called "coverture" was much like the interpretations of Paul's letters in that it gave men authority, and women and children would be under the protection of the man. When you look further into the meaning of the word *kephalē* and Paul's motivation for using it, a different context is apparent. Upon deeper research into the linguistics of Greek language and literature, the term *kephalē* as used by Paul means "kinship, belonging, and connection." Growing up, these principles were fleeting for me, yet I yearned for kinship, belonging, and connection.

I came across the writings of Marg Mowczko and her blog years ago. Part of her ministry focuses on the equality and mutuality of men and women in Christian marriage. In Ephesians 5:25-33, she explains:

The call is for husbands to sacrificially love, care for, and nurture their wives. As Jesus was the source and sustainer of the church, husbands were called to this type of covenant rather than the "head" or "authority" of the wife.

Aha! Looking in the mirror and in my heart, the source and sustainer of and for my life was far from stable. My family dynamic was no different from the traditional patriarchal structure, which had its challenges to create consistent kinship, belonging, and connection. Had my upbringing led me astray?

*Man is never so manly as when he feels deeply, acts boldly, and expresses himself with frankness and with fervor.*

—Benjamin Disraeli, former British Prime Minister

## coach gus' insights

Authority and respect come from serving first and humbling yourself in the process. You are never stronger and more significant than when you become the starting point.

# chapter three

# The Dark Night of My Soul

*There is something wrong with me.*
*I am just not enough.*

When you are deprived of basic relational building blocks, a hole starts to develop in your soul. When authoritarian discipline and mixed signals in communication become the norm, reliance on the only starting point you've ever know becomes extremely difficult. I needed a source of strength, substance, and service for my maturing heart and mind. Desperately, I needed one.

Instead, what I received was an emotional cross to bear. A cross that delivered the opening for the bitter root of shame to surface. And surface it did. It landed like a tornado on a muggy afternoon. The fertile ground of feeling unloved, the willingness to do anything to feel loved, and the failures that coincided with these attempts gave *shame* all that it needed.

*There is something wrong with me. I am just not enough.* This became the story I told myself, and my mind reinforced the story. I became hypersensitive in focusing on my failures and the never ending *you are not enough, Britt* narrative that was a continuous loop in my head and my belief system. Sure enough, I was becoming my thought-enforced failures and shortcomings.

This way of life seemed to help with the cross becoming a little lighter. I could live in self-pity, an overall morose state of existence. I was polite and avoided conflict, and slowly sunk deeper into the pit of shame, while at the same time, I was frozen emotionally and mentally. Yet this conflict that raged

**With so many contradictions happening inside of me, the knots tightened that had bound me for so long.**

within me was a visceral anger that could not be expressed or easily accessed by my conscience mind. If speaking in terms of Freudian psychology, my conflict resided in the Id, the place in my conscience where my basic needs called out to be met.

My basic survival needs were met, yet my developing ego needs were suppressed. A healthy sense of ego can develop when there is a source of strength, substance, and service that places a premium on kinship, connection and belonging thus allowing for the healthy ego to develop in a child. My experience led to anger from a depth that had to be suppressed to keep the peace. There was nothing healthy about how I talked, acted, or felt. I needed an oak tree in my life, which was a mess. *I was a mess.*

**Playing patty cake with my recovery went on for over a year.**

What I could not find in a bottle, a powder, lust, or approval from others was *spirit.* The personal ethos that would not destroy my soul, nor trap me in bondage that would tempt me to go prove how defective I was. In this Hero's Journey to the dark night of my soul, actualization was starting to really set in. The reality that the best way I thought about and executed my life landed me in recovery. The reality was that taking away substances left me with me: not the false me; not the self-condemning me; not the overly-

**I was in a dangerous place: limbo.**

gracious me; and not the conflict-avoidant me. With so many contradictions happening inside of me, the knots tightened that had bound me for so long.

When you get to the point of extreme frustration and hopelessness because you feel like you cannot sort through and access your thoughts and feelings, something must give. Escape was always my answer, but what was supposed to give me relief turned into fuel for a fire that raged. As that fire of shame, extreme pride, fear, and insecurity raged on, I was coming up one year clean and sober. I was facing myself on levels that I had never experienced before. I was starting to get claustrophobic . . . my mind and my heart.

When you are not committed to a way of life, when you do not stand for something, you will fall for anything. Even though I had nothing, was worth nothing, I still was not ready for that next level of kinship, connection, and belonging. With this in my mind, I began to smoke marijuana again while in recovery. Living a double life was familiar and more comfortable than allowing the seeds being spread by *kephalē* (Jesus) to take root.

Playing patty cake with my recovery went on for over a year. I was in a dangerous place: limbo. If I kept going on living in this morass of indifference and stagnation, I would turn again to the spirit of immediate gratification. This spirit included immediate shifts of the mind through drugs and alcohol that could only manufacture the authentic source I so desperately wanted.

*This oak tree and me, we're made of the same stuff.*

—Carl Sagan, astronomer and author of *Pale Blue Dot*

# coach gus' insights

The stories we tell ourselves serve as powerful rein-
forcements of our current reality. Giving yourself a
positive and resilient narrative will help you become
a source of life-giving encouragement for yourself
and others.

# chapter four

# The Missing Links Were Revealed

*I started over ...*
*the moment I darkened the doors of the rooms of recovery.*

A s the good approval seeker that I was, I also wanted to
be loved. When Dad gave me the biography of Mickey
Mantle, the New York Yankees slugging Hall of Famer, I read
about a man that my dad adored. He also fit the story that I
wanted to tell the world about myself. *I wanted to be adored
... I wanted to be a Hall of Famer.* Let me be clear, as I sought
approval, I also loved the Mick and what he did on the ball
field, as a humble superstar. I carry the humility that I played
with today. I carry the competitive spirit into my coaching
profession. In playing the role of humble star, yet living in
the prison of shame, I generously practiced and lived out the
Mick's self-sabotaging tendencies.

Alcohol became a part of my story when I was just 14. By
adding it to my equation, my social capital grew rapidly. I could
hit home runs during the day and drink at night. As a 14 year

old trying to handle this type of behavior, inevitably there was no sustaining it. It became a boom or bust lifestyle. That was what my life had become. There was no middle ground for steady progress, fruits of demanding work, or building a foundation that could sustain the growth necessary that would set roots of integrity, character, and the courage to do what was right for myself.

Doing everything to seek approval can be dangerous too. As a 16 year old, just having two drinks before driving, with a buzz, I decided to race my friend Scott around a local business park. His BMW took the sharp corner like a cheetah grabbing the ground at an extreme angle and accelerating to chase down its kill. My mom's Acura Integra, with less ground grabbing capability, buckled at the difficulty in the turn I was trying to complete. It went spinning in circles and hit a fire hydrant then rested facing the opposite direction. The back wheels were bent underneath the car like the flimsy matchbox car axles that you have seen in so many little boys' toy piles. My wrist was jammed from the steering wheel violently jerking back and forth as the wheels folded under the car.

My friend Brad was in the front passenger seat and exited the car. He was scared. I was scared too, but not because of

**My parents reported the accident.**
*I wondered why?*

what had just happened. No, I was scared because of how much trouble I was going to be in.

The weight of what had just happened did not set in for me or the danger I had put Brad and myself in. I was worried about losing driving privileges, my social credibility, and not having a car to drive. In August of that same year, I had another accident.

This time, I was really drunk and got behind the wheel of Mom's Acura. I dosed off and hit a parked car, then proceeded to run that car into a creek.

My parents reported the accident. *I wondered why?* Somewhere in my mind I thought they were betraying me, when it was incredibly clear that I should not be on the road driving any longer. I would lose my license until my senior year of high school.

> The oak tree stands vibrantly sturdy and wide like the open arms of Jesus that reach as far west as they do east. To endure seasons of violent weather, the oak tree can grow deeper roots . . . roots that can grow as deep as the tree is tall. Projecting strength, substance, and service is one thing, living in this space is quite another. Becoming a starting point, a generative force, in your own life and the lives others, you must start at a deeply conscious and emotional level.
>
> What has taken root because of shame, guilt, disappointment, pain, fear, self-importance, etc., cannot be undone without digging deeper than those roots. It's why many people don't do it. The work of uncovering the misconceptions, discovering the truth, and enduring the inevitable pain it will take to become authentic and real has a degree of difficulty that must provide purpose on the other side. I started over ... the moment I darkened the doors of the rooms of recovery.

On September 18, 2005, I came as close to that manufactured spirit as I ever would again. I had dropped by a friend's house to get a little bit of marijuana and saw the piles of white stuff getting lined up. I ran out of there as fast as I could.

The next day, September 19, would become my clean and sober birthday … one that I have celebrated with relish for the last 16 years as I write *The Oak Tree Source*. *By the Grace of God, I pray, I will celebrate every year for the rest of my life.*

Clean and sober has a meaning that goes far beyond abstaining from mind-altering substances. By becoming sober and willing to do whatever it took to stand for something and allowing myself to be raptured by the love of Jesus, by His blood, I am made clean. I was ready to be a source of strength, substance, and service to myself. As you are. Even though the blood of Jesus made me clean, the work had just begun. The walls around my heart were still thick. As I discovered every day forward, His love and presence are thicker.

Abba, the name for God that connotates "Daddy" was the source I turned to first. Brennan Manning's book *Abba's Child* was recommended to me by a close friend. He also invited me to hear Manning speak in Lafayette, Colorado. It was a revolutionary experience for me.

*I now understand that God was not a figure*
*like my grandfather or the punisher I envisioned him being.*

*I now embraced that He knew me intimately*
*and loved me as a father loves his son.*

My patriarchal examples were powerful, yet not always loving. *Were they for you?* I longed for approval from the male figures in my life. *Did you?* In some ways, that approval seeking persists to this day. *Abba's Child* had a profound effect on me as

I struggled to find an anchor early on in sobriety. It appeared, along with the wisdom of Brennan Manning, at the right time. I'm forever grateful to my friend for opening the door to it.

Armed with a fresh perspective about God, and some comfort knowing that He cared for me more intimately than I thought possible altered the way I thought and acted. Not only did He help me comprehend the source of His love, but He also showed me. He demonstrated it in ways I hadn't conceived of. I became acquainted with

**The transparency and vulnerability that circled the men's groups were inspired by hearts, not physical conquering.**

a group of men through the rooms of recovery that held men's meetings. The starting point was love; the objective was humility. The focus was sharing in an authentic way to create kinship, belonging and connection . . . my missing links.

God showed me how real His love was through the truth of who He is. The men in this group, the core five or six who consistently showed up every week as well as the men who came and went sporadically, helped me lean into healing, understanding, patience, compassion, and love.

Urgency and rest simultaneously permeated the living rooms where we met. An urgency to share good news and insights through prayer and submission to our Abba Father, but restful listening and presence that made the environment safe and trusting. These men had become a starting point for themselves by surrendering to the source. By associating with them, in some ways it felt like I was part of a sports team, rich with loyalty and common purpose. Yet, the transparency and vulnerability that circled the men's groups were inspired by hearts, not physical conquering.

It is critical to be in a fraternity of men who are not afraid to tell you the truth as they see it about you. As a man seeking strength and substance, you must find other men doing the same so that Psalm 27:17 "As iron sharpens iron so one man sharpens another" comes alive in you. There is no greater honor and privilege than men who sacrificially and transparently help one another.

> By inspiring hearts, our minds were changed and integrated so that we each walked in an integrity that was visible from inside of each of us. While physically conquering and exerting your masculine self, it can create power—a power that has limitations. As an aspiring professional athlete, I thrived on conquering opposing tacklers or pitchers who tried to exert their will over me. I confronted a truth: competition brought out the best of me and the worst and most critical of me.

*You seek the heights of manhood when you seek the depths of God.*

—Edwin Louis Cole, Founder of the Christian Men's Network

## coach gus' insights

The beauty of life is that you can start over at any time. Don't worry about your age, what people will think, or what you will miss out on. What matters is that you live a life you can be proud of and a life that gives you fulfillment and satisfaction.

# chapter five

# My Source of Living

*No one could have told me that my greatest failures*
*would help tell the story of my greatest strengths.*

Without a source that I could anchor to, the boom or bust nature of my life would continue for many more years. Source needs three things to anchor to:

1. Honesty

2. Steadfastness

3. True Alignment

These are the anchors that helped me grow in being a source (generative force) that give me strength and substance in my presence like an oak tree.

Honesty can be very painful, and at the same time be the most cathartic endeavor we ever engage in. The more honest I became about my part in every action, every thought, and every emotion, the more I built a character that was steadfast. When the light of honesty broke through the darkness of my pain and shame, it hurt.

Honesty, as in:

- Finally realizing that *I had made the decision* to serve myself at the bar and drink three double margaritas before I had a physical fight with another, leaving me with a broken jaw.

- Finally realizing that *I had made the decision* not to be on time for work to numerous jobs, which resulted in being fired.

These painful decisions and screw ups served to be pieces of a steadfastness building inside of me. I could not have imagined my greatest failures would help tell the story of my greatest strengths. I wouldn't have listened. I wouldn't have believed.

As building a character of steadfastness grew, it became me. I had no choice but to act dutifully and dependably. A sense of purpose . . . that there was kinship, belonging, and association with success and not failure, strength not weakness, and a path to take that would add value to those I met. My purpose ultimately became to spread seeds of love, hope, connection, kinship, and strength. These create substance, which we are all looking for more of.

As you become a source, a starting point, a generative force beginning in your own life, purpose will start to emerge. You can't have generativity without purpose. There must be a "why," an anchor, true alignment within. Jesus had true alignment with His purpose, beliefs, actions, and words. As the source of the church, He challenged an environment that relied on the letter of the law. As a generative force, Jesus brought the spirit of the law to life, a force that could not be denied. He became the starting point that created a focus on fulfillment, not only of scripture but fulfillment of the void and thirst our souls so desperately craved.

When you figure out what you believe in and what you want to stand for, your fulfillment and purpose will be revealed in connection with your spirit. Becoming a source of strength and substance for others will lead you onto the path to fulfillment. It will, in turn, lead you to the generating force of your purpose. Imitating the life of Jesus Christ has quenched my thirst and solidified strong roots in me. He will for you too.

As a boy going to Saint Thomas Moore Church, I was captivated by the stations of the cross. Each held my attention much more than the homily and ritual of the Catholic Church. I would gaze around the stations, watching what looked to be the cross become heavier in each image. I was mesmerized with the types of graphics and carvings that were used by the artist who created it.

I identified with those scenes on a real level. In turn, I believed that I needed to carry a cross like Jesus did. When what I really needed at that time was *Dona Nobis Pacem*, the Latin phrase for *Grant Us Peace*. By carrying the cross of my family's hurts, peace was not something that could accompany that cross.

At the time, I didn't realize that Jesus granted me peace after I let him carry the cross. When the seeds he was spreading started to take root in me, I could rest in His loving arms. Finding peace and rest allowed me to be "okay" if only for a mo-

**The tools that I had as a young boy weren't the best.**

ment. I spent so much time agonizing over the past and anxiety ridden over the future that the moment I lived in had no chance to blossom into opportunity and invitation. "Okay" meant I wasn't in fight, flight, or freeze mode. I froze so often being in the middle of arguments and trying to cover Dad's tracks while agonizing over Mom's fear of the places we had been.

- ✓ I froze when my grandfather tried to get me to drink alcohol, so he, my dad, and I could talk about me and what I was struggling with.
- ✓ I froze when my 10th grade world history teacher told me that I was the biggest asshole he had ever taught.
- ✓ I froze when an angry husband came to our home and punched Dad in the mouth for the affair Dad was having with his wife.

The ability to fight left me after I punched my father's friend in the balls because he was taking my dad away again. Dad still left with him. I was never a runner. I always confronted the issue, the conflict directly. The tools that I had as a young boy weren't the best. For a long time, I could not do anything about the verbal abuse that was hurled at me. I would stand and take the abuse, whatever it was.

This was MY cross and the best way I could figure to deal with it ended in destruction, usually my own. *Dona Nobis Pacem* takes on a new meaning when despite your best efforts, you cannot create this for yourself. The greatest gift you can ever receive is "peace granted to you." The tension, stress, demands, pain, suffering of the world give you—us—the ultimate invitation to choose to let the source *Dona Nobis Pacem*.

There is no amount of money, beauty, power, or material goods that can give you what your soul longs for. Emptiness

pervades these pursuits. Deception pervades these pursuits.
Each is led by pride and greed. Apart from the source, seeds
of discord, discontent, anger, frustration, distress and worry are
sowed. Paul explains in his main point in the passage from the
Book of Colossians 1:15-18, granting peace, *kephalē*, shows that
Jesus is the creator, origin, and beginning of everything in the
universe. This includes Jesus being the "author" of the Church.

Paul used the word *kephalē* (head) in this context—the
context of origin and beginning, or, as some say "source" infus-
ing the seeds of harmony, unity, love, serenity, calm, still, and
purpose. These were the seeds that were planted in me 16 years
ago. When I quit carrying my cross and allowed the author of
my story to carry it, His seeds were taking root and substance
began to fill and flow from them.

That strength and substance were moving me toward the
purpose of my life. The gentle nudge from a loving God plus
the substance of my life changing and gaining strength sent me
to the upheaval of my shame. It happened in middle school.

As a student, my world changed dramatically when I was
enrolled in a new school district at a new level, one that was
more affluent than my previous school. I wore a jean jacket with
heavy metal pins on it, such as Iron Maiden, Ozzy Osbourne,
Metallica, etc. But I was an athlete. I was special, or so I thought.

Athletes at West Middle School did not wear heavy metal-
ladened jackets. Even though they listened to the music, they
were preppy in their appearance. In gym class, my radius striped
socks were worn up to my knees, as I did in elementary school.
I almost felt naked walking out that first day of gym class. Boys
were looking at me and snickering at each other. I stuck out like
a sore thumb walking out of the locker room.

I could have frozen again because insecurity and hyper self-awareness were raging inside to my core. But I didn't freeze. This time, I connected to a source—unknown to me at the time—and that source was one of my anchors: steadfastness. During those years, as difficult as they were, a sense of duty to connect and create belonging became the most important part of my life. For better or worse, a steadfastness in building relationships was my focus.

**When authenticity meets your gifts, the urge to impress and seek approval falls away.**

As the boys snickered, I moved toward a few of them to connect. We ended up talking about sports and one kid graciously suggested I wear my socks around my ankles to take the focus off of me. There was certainly a degree of approval seeking in that steadfastness, being the new kid at school trying to break into social cliques that had been established for many years at the elementary school level—none of which I had belonged to. My main avenue to connect and build relationships was always sports. The honest and pure me shined through when I could play and use the gifts God gave me. His light shined through me. God delights in watching his kids shine the light He has put in them. I never felt freer and more focused than on the ball field.

When authenticity meets your gifts, the urge to impress and seek approval fall aways. You become attractive in a way that is true. This truth of who I was as an athlete would help me express myself in a way that was pure. And it helped me connect and associate with many of the boys at West Middle School. They could see my passion for sports and my natural talent. Yet it didn't always mean I was accepted. There was the eighth grade baseball pitcher, a class ahead of me, who wanted to pick a fight because I proclaimed that I could throw a ball at 70 miles per hour in 7th grade—which I could. Or the eighth grader who hid my new Avia high top basketball shoes and tied them in knots around a locker opening. It took me an hour to undo them.

Competition breeds the greatness of who one is, and the worst of who one isn't. Just as I wanted to be king of the mountain when I wrestled my dad as a little boy, I wanted to be validated if I was the best athlete in school. That lack of val-idation would exist in me for many, many

**The only passing grade I was looking at was becoming a first class victim.**

years. I began to feel like Jekyll and Hyde. On the ball field, I was free to be me. Off the field, the angry, scared, searching for validation me bubbled up.

School started to become a struggle for me. Elementary school was not difficult, but middle school was a different story. I was so lost and alone in a sea of middle schoolers. I was not organized as a student. When I started to fall behind in classes, my old friend shame came knocking. In full force, the inner voice roared and accused me of all the things that I believed to be true:

*You aren't smart enough, Britt.*
*Britt, you are too stupid to pass this class.*
*You will never understand that equation, Britt.*
*Britt, you are so dumb.*
*You know everyone is much smarter than you.*

Shame became relentless. I had no defense against it as I felt worse and worse about plummeting grades and missed assignments. The simplest of actions was to turn in the assignments. The combination of pride and shame made it nearly impossible to humble myself to turn and ask for help and at the same time complete the work to help fight off shame. The only passing grade I was looking at was becoming a first class victim. It was more comfortable. How horrible is that to admit? With no way out and no help coming, I let those falling grades and missing assignments be gas for the shame fire that was raging. The victim mentality, albeit more comfortable because it was what I knew and had lived for a long time, was tearing me apart slowly on the inside.

Living this contradiction of victim in the classroom and at home and hero in sports couldn't coexist. It was only sustainable and able to be masked for short periods until breakdowns and acting out in numerous ways became more prevalent. The one thing that I held sacred—athletics—started to get caught in the blaze. Drinking before practice, not practicing hard, and not staying in great physical condition became my new norm. The one place where I reveled mounted pressure on me.

Never giving an inch, I believed I had what it took to come through when asked, but now I was succumbing to the pain of the war between my pride and my shame. By my sophomore year in high school with all the sabotage and battle going on within, I found myself as the 4th place hitter on the best high school baseball team in the biggest classification in Colorado. Even though it was my first varsity baseball game, I was relaxed and confident.

Two springs earlier, my dad had taken me to a Cherry Creek varsity baseball game. As I watched, I thought *these eighteen year olds were not any better than me.* I was fourteen. At sixteen, I found myself stepping into the batter's box for my first at bat, at that same field my dad had taken me to two years earlier. I was the "next up—and—coming star" at Cherry Creek High School. I got a high fastball, a pitch I loved to hit. I got under it just a smidge and popped the ball into left center field. With those jitters out of the way, my next two at bats showed my power. I hit that same high fastball over the left center field wall. The next bat, the left handed pitcher went with the curveball that I saw right out of his hand. With my swing, I launched it over the left field wall. It was a surprisingly great day for my first varsity baseball game!

The next day, a fastball came right down the middle to me. I sent the ball soaring over the center field wall. Three straight at bats with a home run had the scouts buzzing in the crowd. Later that year, I would miss two games because I was ineligible to play. My grades were dismal. My coach and the team started to lose their trust in me.

Coming off an all-state campaign my junior year and being the quarterback of a state championship football team, expectations were sky high going into the playoffs my senior year. Sixty feet and a few inches away from me was a curveball throwing right hander. The relaxed and confident ball player of two years ago had been replaced by an anxious player, pressing to achieve, who could not sit on that curveball. My Jekyll and Hyde persona had resurfaced. We lost that day and did not advance in the state tournament.

*The men who have the right ideals . . . are those who
have the courage to strive for the happiness which
comes only with labor and effort and self-sacrifice,
and those whose joy in life springs in part from power
of work and sense of duty.*

—Teddy Roosevelt, 26th U.S. president

## coach gus' insights

Your attitudes, beliefs, and thoughts must line
up with your speech and actions in order to lead.
People will follow you if your insides match your
outside.

# chapter six

# What Is My Role?

*Living in the world between pride and shame*
*didn't allowed me to stay firmly planted*
*in the day I was living.*

I cry as I write this because of opportunities missed, and the choices I made that altered the course of my life. As I was writing *The Oak Tree Source*, the documentary "The Last Dance" about the 1998 Chicago Bulls was airing. As I watch the episode on Michael Jordan's gambling habits, Jordan said, "I don't have a gambling problem. I have a competition problem."

Even though I was not a gambler, I gambled plenty with my reckless behavior trying to illicit reaction and approval. I can, though, relate to competing as if my life depended on it. As that competitiveness burned inside of me, I was embarrassed by letting that slow curveball pitcher get the best of me in the state tournament my senior year. I was unbelievably humiliated when we got shut out in our Homecoming football game. Not only was I mortified that I threw three interceptions, but I was disgusted by the way my team was physically dominated.

As we gathered for the post-game meeting in the end zone, I walked to the other end of the field and sat in a snowbank looking up into the hazy clouds vowing to never let this happen again.

And it didn't.

I went on to have a five touchdown to one interception ratio in four playoff games including a state championship win. Then, my dark side reentered. My competitive spirit was always a trusted asset, until it wasn't. It quickly became a detriment to my mental, emotional, and spiritual well-being. The harder I tried to walk between two worlds, the more difficult it became to keep the train on the track.

My high school career ended. I graduated with an unimpressive 1.4 grade point average. I was glad they didn't announce it as my name was called to take the ceremonious walk across the stage to receive my diploma.

Humiliating as it was, it was fitting for me so I could reinforce the narrative I had told myself for many years. The story we tell ourselves may be the most powerful motivator or most powerful roadblock to breakthrough we ever experience. My story of shame, disappointment, missed opportunities, self-loathing, became a self-fulfilling prophecy, which was the worst thing that could have happened for me.

I always thought I would make it to the big leagues because I was talented and would put in "just enough" work. "Just enough" work gets you a seat at the table with unfilled potential and the triplets: *should've*, *could've*, and *would've*. Living in the world between pride and shame didn't allow me to stay firmly planted in the day I was living. I heard it put this way in recovery:

*If you've got one foot in yesterday*
*and one foot in tomorrow,*
*you are pissing all over today.*

That was me.

For the first time, I realized what becoming a source of strength and substance for myself and others could mean for men everywhere. With Jesus Christ as my source, with his Kingdom as the foundation building inside of me, my presence will be steadfast, solid, noble, honorable, and true. With the God of the Universe spirit living inside of me, my finite presence becomes connected **I could have walked out, not facing the reconstruction of my soul that had already begun.** to the infinite. When you become the starting point, the generating force for yourself and others through discipline and service, traits such as honorable, steadfast, noble, reliable, and sturdy like an oak tree are how you will be known.

Now, when I look out over the landscape that presents itself in modern male culture, I see the traditional view of masculinity under fire. You may as well. Those traits include being the breadwinner of the household and carrying the prestige that goes with it. Others include discipline, logic, rational, and competitiveness.

In "Understanding Men and Masculinity in Modern Society," Flourish Itula-Abumere reveals findings on masculinity done by multiple authors in the late 1970s and mid-1980s where the term "Sturdy Oak" was associated with typical male masculinity. I would argue that the "Sturdy Oak" is as uncommon as the trait of male masculinity. If you pair

the metaphor of the Oak Tree with the powerful truth
that the life of Jesus Christ gives us, there is a way of life
that merges traditional male qualities with those that
have been associated with femininity: intuition, empa-
thy, nurturing, emotion, and compassion. The renowned
author Earnest Hemingway captured this uncommon
integration:

> The best people possess a feeling for beauty, the
> courage to take risks, the discipline to tell the
> truth, the capacity for sacrifice. Ironically, their
> virtues make them vulnerable; they are often
> wounded, sometimes destroyed.

As traditional gender roles keep changing, you may be
asking the question, "What is my role?" I found myself asking
this same question. God gave me the blessing of my lifetime
with my wife, Carrie. Her blessing on my life is eternal. The
introspection, unlearning, shaping, and molding on God's
potting wheel, the searing truth of my insecurity and fear
were front and center every day early in our marriage. Early
on, I knew a partner like Carrie only comes around once in a
lifetime. I could have walked out, not facing the reconstruction
of my soul that had already begun. I pointed the finger at
Carrie, only to realize there were three fingers pointing back
at me. Those three fingers have always been pride, shame, and
condemnation.

I had come to a place in my life where the pain of living
with those emotions was outweighed by love, acceptance, and
a deep yearning to live with joy and purpose. Understanding
that the catharsis of my life was about to be thrust into hyper
drive, my pride and shame were tested as never before. I asked,
"What is my role?"

I was not okay with my role in our family dynamic, even though "my role" allowed me to go back to school; to chase the dream of coaching football at the highest level; and be a "Sturdy Oak" for my children. How was I to live in a way that is pure, that stands apart from what the world tells men they need to be?

> *To be still and know that He is God.*
> —Psalm 46:10

It became clear to me: The pride, shame, and condemnation I carried for most of my life were not going to go away without a fight. After our first child Isabel was born, I made the decision to go back to school. Carrying a full load of classes at night, I took care of Isabel during the day while Carrie built her career in the financial service industry as an executive vice president at Fairway Independent Mortgage where she built a large organization. Fairway is one of the top three mortgage lenders in the United States. Carrie was also an investment manager with Northwestern Mutual.

Today, she has started her own mortgage company called Aslan Home Lending. She is assertive, incredibly intelligent, and tells it like she sees it. Carrie has been to the top of corporate America and helped small businesses alike. Her heart for people is something to behold. She is the first one to lend a helping hand and give her all to those in need. Couple these strong qualities with a loving, compassionate, joyful personality and attitude, I am one blessed man to call Carrie my wife.

Yet, with all these blessings surrounding me, the question continued to arise, "What is my role?" My pride craved the first position as breadwinner, being at company awards dinners and receiving awards, traveling for business, networking, etc., like Carrie did. Conversely, my shame saw these men receiving awards and shaking hands with the leaders of businesses. Through the shame lens, I compared myself to them. I never measured up in the comparison game. It was evident that I was not comfortable in my role as caretaker.

I grew up in the era of ass kickers like Sylvester Stallone, Arnold Schwarzenegger, Mel Gibson, with shades of the Cowboy way a la John Wayne. Before Carrie and I were together, she once got me a birthday card with the John Wayne quote:

**I have always been someone who wanted immediate gratification.**

"If you've got them by the balls their hearts and minds will follow." The quote speaks perfectly to masculinity as most men traditionally know it. I thought I needed to be John Wayne. *I wanted to be John Wayne.* How could I walk in his boots when I was taking care of babies and writing papers, and not wheeling and dealing, selling and closing?

In these moments of comparison, shame, pride, I couldn't understand that the gentle nudge to live with purpose and live with authentic obedience is so much more rewarding than "wheeling and dealing." Obedience can be seen as limiting or dull. Yet, obedience is the key to freedom of mind, body, and spirit. Obedience develops discipline. It takes discipline to live by a set of values and virtues that promotes and develops your purpose. The rewards of living with discipline and obedience are the substance of life.

I have always been someone who wanted immediate gratification. The suddenness of sports always provided it; alcohol
and drugs provided it briefly. Then it turned into a chase for
that perfect high that always ended with more searching. I saw
the men that Carrie worked with as instant successes brimming
with confidence. The truth: I didn't really know anything about
them. Yet, I compared myself to them and thought in some
instances that Carrie would be better off with one of them
instead of me.

Through all the redemptive healing that happened within
me because of finishing my undergraduate degree and getting
a master's degree in education, the hole inside of me was still
wide open with fear, uncertainty, and lack of confidence. To be
a starting point instead of an ending point, there must be discovery, discerning, and discarding of those behaviors, thoughts,
and emotions that hold you back. My discerning and discarding
phase was showing progress. I had not arrived at the mountain
top . . . at least not yet. There was still much work to do. This
was another step in the process that would ultimately lead to
growing stronger roots in my purpose.

If you find yourself thinking you have arrived, you are in
danger of missing miracles. There is always more growth and
development to be had. I find this concept exhilarating. Do not
let your hunger and determination to learn go away. Your ability
to keep setting strong roots of substance and strength will grow
your legacy like a majestic oak tree.

You cannot be a source of life ... one that gives encouragement, love, and strength and leads to a purpose led satisfaction
that is rooted deep in your heart ... without going to those places

inside that scare you or keep you from growing through the pain. This is where essential strength comes from. It allows you to carry more than your share of the human load within relationships, teams, etc. It is GOD STRENGTH.

What God created in me was His substance, His significance. It is my job to spread those seeds like Jesus Christ did. When those seeds of significance grow, God promises man:

> *Make our sons in their prime like sturdy oak trees.*
> —Psalm 144:12

When you become a source of strength, substance, and life-giving encouragement, you enter a purposeful satisfaction. Purposeful satisfaction is the intentional action of doing the work it takes to become available, free, and commanding of your environment. In Genesis, the God of the Universe declares,

> *It is so good, so exceptionally good.*
> *It was evening, it was morning day six.*
> —Genesis 1:31

What did God do on the seventh day? He rested; He enjoyed His creation. As you go through the valleys, the hurts, the hang ups in life, and if you concentrate on being a source of life-giving encouragement, strength, and substance, you can enjoy what He built in you, in any circumstance.

*Adversity toughens manhood, and the characteristic of the good or the great man is not that he has been exempt from the evils of life, but that he has surmounted them.*   —Patrick Henry

## coach gus' insights

The moment you realize that your pride is keeping you from personal development and creating the life you want, the redemptive roots of Jesus Christ will begin to take hold if you ask Him.

# 2 Strength

David strengthened himself with trust in his God.

1 Samuel 30:6

# chapter seven

# Authentic Strength vs Phony Strength

*Authentic strength is so attractive to those that see it.*
*It becomes the benchmark for others to follow*
*when the going gets tough.*

My family and I were watching the latest edition of the *Rocky Balboa* series, "Creed" and "Creed 2." The son of Apollo Creed, Adonis Creed carries on the boxing tradition of the Creed and Balboa families with Rocky serving as his trainer. As I watched, I traveled back to when I first saw the *Rocky* movies as a kid. Rocky Balboa was the embodiment of strength, not only physical strength but resilience, courage, fortitude, grit, and bravery. I got goosebumps every time Rocky would make a fierce comeback in his fights, and ultimately prevail. My "kid mind" told me: If I'm to be considered strong, I must win … right?

As I was writing this book, I also taught Honors American Government at the high school level to juniors. One of the modules is on the concept of civic virtues—contending that when living in a democracy, each has a virtuous responsibility to devote time and talent as a free individual who is living in our democratic republic. A key virtue is integrity.

American culture has a myriad of examples of courage, virtue, bravery, and fortitude. The United States was built on these attributes of strength. In my mind, when it comes to building strength, there are two virtues that stand out and are vitally important:

1. *Perseverance* is the ability to choose the right path and stay with it even when the right path is not popular, or opposition is met.

2. *Contribution* is often thought of as a gift or payment. There's more to it. Your contribution to society depends on your discovering and using your unique gifts and abilities that can be shared with society for the greater good.

In 1783, George Washington was facing a coup from his troops during the Revolutionary War as they battled with Congress over pay. At that time, Congress could not levy taxes. Washington showed his strength in an extraordinary way combining those two virtues. As the story goes, Washington put on his glasses, something that no one had seen him do in public before. He went on to remark,

> Gentlemen, you will permit me to put on my spectacles, for I have not only grown gray, but almost blind in the service of my country.

When Washington's soldiers heard this selfless and vulnerable statement, they dropped their grievance to Congress and continued to fight the war that led to the creation of the United States. Washington's modeling of a virtuous act exhibited authentic strength. Authentic strength is so attractive to those that see or hear it, it becomes the benchmark for others to follow when the going gets tough. For some, it may not be obvious when there is not much at stake, or their motives are not grounded in virtue.

> There's also a phony strength—a pretend and braggy strength—sometimes with nuggets of truth but woven with elements of untruths. Raising its head too often, the focus is on self, immediate gratification, and boasting of accomplishments—sometimes exaggerated. I know these phony strengths well when I was quite the buzzkill whirling in my rants. More times than not, you could find me sitting at a bar with friends.

My friends were raving about their exploits with women.

I was in the extreme. Anything that I believed to be *a truth*, I boasted that it was the only truth—telling my friends, and myself, that getting high and drunk was phony, not authentic. That wasn't the truth. The only truth was in the authenticity of a relationship, something that was phony and nonexistent as we sat at the bar BSing.

One of my sponsors told me, "We are all looking for *spirit*. Why do you think alcohol is referred to as 'wine and spirits'?"

My new truth became: *I was looking for authenticity in all of the wrong places.*

Throughout human history alcohol has been used as a medical treatment and an elixir to bring about spirit. This manufactured strength builder had the exact opposite effect on me for almost 20 years. Manufacturing strength starts to corrode your soul.

I was never the boastful type, but I certainly had my moments of firing back on the ball field when I was challenged. That's when I was utterly self-absorbed. Typically, most think being self-absorbed is when someone is concerned about material possessions, how they look, money, etc. My self-absorption came from how much and how often could I blow myself up and degrade myself ... because I was not good enough. Something was wrong with me.

I was in search of authentic strength for so long. But it was something I didn't find until I came to the end of myself. And at the end of me was the merciful and loving spirit of Jesus Christ. Just like the night I cried out to Him when I thought my heart was going to explode after snorting too much cocaine, and *He* prompted me to get up and call 911. Jesus met me in my deepest shame and darkness because He is strength authentically personified.

**I lay on the ground writhing in physical, mental, emotional, and spiritual pain.**

*What is essential strength?* Every human being is given a physique that possesses muscle so that one's body will operate the way it is supposed to. Your physique is a beautiful gift given to you by God. It plays an essential part in your development over time.

*Do you have to feed your physique?*

Yes, you do.

*Do you have to build your muscles continuously for them to be adequate in the operation of your physical self?*

No, you do not.

There are behaviors that go beyond your physical fitness that are more important and tell the story of essential strength. Most regular human activity allows your muscles to grow and sustain you in everyday life. It is obvious that athletes of any kind rely on their physique as an essential part of **My spirit** their performance. Being an athlete for many years **was crushed.** myself, the difference in building physical strength translated to better play, a healthier body, and more endurance. Every day I engage in a regular weight training routine.

At 31, I broke. Housesitting for my father, I had spent the previous afternoon playing, drinking, and drugging. I had consumed all the liquor in the house and emptied my bindle of cocaine. The next morning found me spread out in his foyer, writhing in physical, mental, emotional, and spiritual pain. Finally gaining consciousness, I wasn't sure I had any strength, let alone essential strength.

*Essential strength.*

Yet somewhere inside of me there still existed resolve, and even more importantly, hope. If I still had breath in my body, and an ounce of will power, I was going to get up again. The sciatic nerve pain in my lower back, hip, and right leg persisted for a few days after I had been broken again. My spirit was crushed. I was a hollow shell of a person. With nowhere to turn, I entered the "last house on the block" as old timers in recovery like to call it. What felt like crawling with my tail between my legs, with shame raging, and pride reduced to a murmur, I took a seat and started the journey to build essential strength.

*Authentic strength.*

That beginning meant accepting the fact that the way I did things was not working. Admitting that the way I used alcohol and drugs was killing me was not as difficult this time. It had been five years since I had first walked into a meeting of Alcoholics Anonymous. There was no one coming to pick me up; there was no one coming to bail me out. I had to face myself: the fears, the heartbreaks, the failures, the lethal combination of pride and shame that destroys.

But ... this time was different. I had my hero walking with me.

When there are so many layers and complexities to your experiences, your beliefs, what you've learned, the virtue of patience becomes the ultimate strength builder. I was not going to be that authoritative and confident person that I was as a state champion quarterback.

I was going to be stronger than I had ever been, and more authentic than I had ever been. Hope was restored in me, and my personality would lead to positivity and energy.

My hero was walking along beside me.

*Authenticity is everything! You have to wake up every day and look in the mirror and you want to be proud of the person looking back at you. You can only do that if you are being honest with yourself and being a person of a high character. You have an opportunity every single day of your life to write that story.* —Aaron Rodgers, Green Bay Packers quarterback

## coach gus' insights

When there is hope, there is help. And when you step away from the phoniness that surrounds so many of us, the help will appear: sometimes subtly; sometimes with a sledgehammer.

# chapter eight

# Beginning the Hero's Journey

*When I started to see myself as the "hero" of the journey,*
*the hero I so desperately needed, strength took on new meaning.*

Journeys have steps. Some are big; others are small. Yet each is essential. Your walk through the Hero's Journey will do that. It doesn't happen all at once. Get ready to test every ounce of your positivity and energy.

## Step One … Honesty with Self

There were many days when my emotions got the best of me, and I would become over emotional. As I started to understand the basics of self-centeredness, control, and my part in every decision in my life, autonomy of mind, body, and soul started to develop and take root.

I was open and honest about everything. Sometimes my zealous drive to create a new authentic me … to open up … backfired and was used against me. But I persevered, knowing that there would be arrows out there and that all would not enthusiastically embrace this new me.

Finally, my authentic strength was allowed to surface. When the phony strength attempted to enter, the door was slammed in its face.

My acorn seed was starting to bud inside, tended to by Jesus Christ. The strength of AA meetings and the wounded healers in those rooms were a foundation of accountability. The wisdom and experience that poured through those meetings was transcendent.

The more I read AA's *Big Book*, the more I saw myself in those pages. When people shared their experience, strength, and hope at meetings, I trusted them and found common emotional and spiritual ground with them. Even though essential strength is built in solitude and trial, the shared healing and wisdom of those who are farther along on the journey than we are can never be discounted. This is why mentorship, teaching, and coaching are so important. It doesn't matter if it is the Boys and Girls Club or a multinational corporation. If we are not actively passing on lived experience to help others, whatever strength we have built will never become essential.

**When I started to see myself as the hero of the journey, strength took on new meaning.**

The journey of my life, and in so many instances, my perceived weaknesses lead the way. When I started to see myself as the Hero of the journey—my journey … the hero I so desperately needed—strength took on new meaning.

Joseph Campbell theories revealed in his books, *The Hero with a Thousand Faces* and *The Power of Myth*, have been mirrored by a wide variety of artists and writers. Even acclaimed storyteller and producer George Lucas credits Campbell's work as an influencer for the *Star Wars* saga. In an interview with Bill Moyers, Campbell remarked as to why he chose to write about the Hero's Journey, saying . . .

> . . . because that's what's worth writing about. I mean, even in popular novel writing, you see, the main character is the hero or heroine, which is to say, someone who has found or achieved or done something beyond the normal range of achievement and experience. A hero is someone who has given his life to something bigger than himself or other than himself.

To be a hero, you must be willing to lose yourself to your purpose, the purpose that is something bigger than yourself. It's the first step in the transition to become an Oak Tree. This initial step begins your walk to becoming your own hero. It allows you to step into the bigger story that brings significance to your life.

Make no mistake: Doing something or achieving something beyond the normal range of experience does not have to be the most grandiose thing you can think of.

When you make the decision to obey your own hero, stepping into the bigger story, what you are made for is revealed . . . THIS IS ENOUGH! For most of my life, I thought I had to be superhuman to be loved, to gain acceptance, to belong. When, what I needed was to be my own hero.

Essential strength is the byproduct. What does it mean to be your own hero? I had built a life on the counterproductive duo of pride and shame. There was nothing in between the two.

There was no being okay because my experience showed me that there had to be crisis or kingdom. Living life on life's terms was not an option that was usually practiced or encouraged.

## Step Two ... Replanting

When I had no other choice but to live life on life's terms, the uncovering of my discontent was not hard to find. The sledge-hammer came for me. Not willing to escape my thoughts and emotions any longer, I sat with them. I sat with the pain of not becoming a major league ball player; the fact that I could not save my parents' marriage; and being too drunk to defend myself ... suffering a broken jaw as the consequence.

> It is amazing how you can use your strength for things that take it away and take away the things that will give you strength.

The second part of becoming an Oak Tree is the willingness to start over, to be replanted. During my uncovering process, which is still happening, the ability to feel and let go of the hurts and hang ups was crucial.

To continue the Hero's Journey, Campbell points out,

> ...and then to get out of that posture of dependency, psychological dependency, into one of psychological self-responsibility, requires a death and resurrection, and that is the basic motif of the Hero's Journey, Leaving one condition, finding the source of life to bring you forth in a richer or more mature or other condition.

You must let go of the behaviors, thoughts, and actions that don't benefit you any longer. Dependence can be an ugly word if used in the sense of neediness, approval, and recognition and the fear of abandonment. The practice of discarding thought patterns that no longer suit you is a painful process that is vital to building essential strength and becoming an Oak Tree. When you are gripped by fear and the unhealthy dependence on people, place, and things, the ability to build essential strength is blunted by the energy it takes to keep up the dependence. It is amazing how you can use your strength for things that take it away and take away the things that will give you strength.

I could not live the Jekyll and Hyde lifestyle anymore. To enable the resurrection in me to take place, this paradox in me had to die. Nine years into my marriage and responsible and sober living, I was firmly seeded with my roots as an Oak Tree.

My journal entry on December 26th read,

> *The greatest gift I've been given is the unconditional love and expectation of nothing but to be myself. No need to perform; no need to seek approval. But … what do I do? Perform, seek approval, try to be something I'm not. I am in enough pain that I cannot stay here. Thank you for moving me off my mark, Father.*

*If you're going through hell, keep going.*

—Winston Churchill

## coach gus' insights

When you've been through significant challenges and make it back, there is a confidence and surety you have about yourself that can never be taken away.

# chapter nine

# Letting Go

*Stepping directly into the Refiner's Fire with abandon,*
*with no regard for anything but to seat the roots of strength,*
*substance, and legacy was the only choice.*

On the road to building the strength of a hero, to become a source of strength, substance, and life-giving encouragement is a process. My unhealthy dependencies have taken deep root and have been nourished well. It will take time to discard them. Responsibility broken down to its root words are "response" and "able." As a result of undergoing my own version of a resurrection, I became *response-able* when I discovered those unhealthy dependencies no longer served who I was becoming.

## Step THREE … Letting Go

The concept of "letting go" is so powerful. Yet, it takes the Hero's Journey to connect with the source. Most days, I am quite grateful for the journey. The realization that I must be my own hero to build strength in my character, so that I act with an integrity that becomes who I am, and when the question arises inside of me to act in any other way than with integrity, my condition of character does not allow it. After getting a taste of essential strength and authentic integrity, I realize I was made for it! As a result, I need to share this gift.

Bill Moyers shares Campbell's comments on this step,

Leaving one condition, finding the source of life to bring you forth in a richer or more mature or other condition.

In becoming an oak tree, your strength becomes rich and filled with substance that shows in your presence. Maturity and the "other" condition because of becoming your own hero are the "Refiner's Fire."

*The crucible is for silver, and the furnace is for gold,*
*and the Lord tests hearts.*
—Proverb 17:3

The test of your heart is never more refining than when you are in close relationship with someone else. *I want gold; I do not want silver.* To truly experience the *other*, the journey that brings the crescendo to your Hero's Journey, go to the depths of yourself that you did not know existed.

For me, stepping directly into the Refiner's Fire with abadon, **The Refiner's Fire was becoming unbearable.** with no regard for anything but to seat the roots of strength, substance, and legacy, was the only choice. I began writing only to keep a journal so I could diffuse the power my thoughts had over me.

Journaling became part of my process. What I discovered was that my story needed to be told. As I journaled it seemed like my emotional and mental state became worse. The Refiner's Fire was becoming unbearable. My journal entry from January 12 reveals:

> ...*pushing myself past my limits again. I am suspicious though. Carrie got home from Vegas at midnight. Her text went off. I always question that in the early hours. What do I fill the trust gap with? Trust or suspicion? I will stay in attachment and not love if I don't replace suspicion with trust.*

Before my marriage, suspicion reigned in me for years. But it never surfaced the way it did until I got married. There was much to lose. When the stakes become high, this is when you see how deep your roots are.

**I could not see, what I could not see.**

To be an *Oak Tree Source*, you must be willing to be tested, tested by all the elements that can harm you. This way you know that your source is honest, steadfast, and true. On February 9, I wrote,

> ... *will this insecurity ever end? It is so disheartening to know that this fear and insecurity is still so present in me. After all the work I've done and what seemed to be God's intention in this burden has turned out to be elusive.*

I could not see, what I could not see. With the unfounded suspicion of my marriage, I trusted that God was going to bring me through the fire and turn me into gold. The accuser, the enemy, the devourer had me believing in the self-fulfilling prophecy.

> An *Oak Tree Source* trusts that no matter what happens externally, it's roots, foundation, and nourishment will stand strong in adverse conditions. The strength that arises out of the Hero's Journey is nothing short of miraculous. Heroes captivate most because of their amazing feats of supernatural power and abilities, and that they defeat the enemy. Yet, how much more meaningful is the story of a hero who overcomes the enemy within, to be the person he or she was meant to be, and to live the purpose that was meant for his or her life?
>
> It takes strength and courage to start over, to pull the roots you had, and let someone else replant you. When that someone who replants you is the God of the Universe, strength takes on a whole new meaning.

The chase for temporal strength and social capital left me with a hole that could not be filled with what the world had to offer. Eternal strength led me to the source. In turn, it led me to become the *Oak Tree Source*. Eternity is made clear through the Refiner's Fire, when you have nowhere else to turn, when you have exhausted all the strength you can muster, you become open and willing. Even the greatest of heroes needs

**It takes strength and courage to start over, to pull the roots you had, and let someone else replant you.**

help along the journey. Superman needed Lois Lane to continue to encourage him. Jesus Christ had the wonderful support and love of His Mother Mary, and Mary Magdalene. And I needed a trusted advisor, confidant, and truth teller. Marc Miller was this for me.

In my journal entry March 11, I wrote:

*I am seeing Marc Miller tomorrow for the first time in
many years. As I think about what to talk to him about
my mind runs on …*

- *Men who like Carrie's Facebook Posts*
- *Does she intentionally not get back to me?*
- *Is this all fear?*
- *Fear of older men.*
- *Fear of men 6 feet and taller.*
- *Confides in other men rather than me.*
- *My place, my role.*
- *Giving Carrie too much power in our marriage.*
- *Will I ever get free?*
- *Fear is racing in my head right now.*

God had turned the furnace to "full blast," or so it seemed.
I continued with a journal entry on March 20:

*Obsession: If she doesn't sit next to me when we pray, is
something going on? If she doesn't add an exclamation
point after the "I love you" text, does she really mean it?*

*And on … and on … and on …. Will it ever end? I
know you are real and present with me, Father! Why do
I continue to dwell on these suspicions? Part of me wants
to give up.*

Yes, God had turned the furnace up to "full blast" and the shame and insecurity were searing as they held on while being burned out of me. Sometimes all you can do is "hold on to your ass" and not make things worse, I journaled. I laughed at all the times I made it worse. There were plenty. Becoming an *Oak Tree Source* takes discipline and discernment to really breakthrough the veil of fear and anxiety and how either can manifest physically, which makes holding on that much more difficult.

There have been times where I had such a physical reaction to an interaction I encountered between my wife and another

**I no longer dread carrying my own weight.**

man, I thought I was going to throw up. I went through physical withdrawals early in my marriage from the emotional baggage I carried from decades of shame, performance, approval seeking, and pride.

And I knew that I wanted to be *whole* more than I wanted to be sick. I knew that marrying a confident, accomplished, compassionate, and strong woman was what I wanted. God knew where this union was going to take the two of us. In all my troubles and struggles, I always saw the image of the stations of the cross, which gave me hope, when it seemed like hope was lost. At the point when I knew the difference, I was never going to settle for less than God's best for me! The mega popular rock band Pearl Jam has a short ballad called "Wasted Reprise." The opening goes, *Having faced a life wasted, I'm never going back.*

That was me. I didn't want to be wasted. And I didn't want to regress.

One of my dear, life-long friends Peyton Garnsey mentioned this to me years ago, escaping a life wasted has built weight-carrying capacity and strength. I no longer dread carrying my own weight but relish the fact that I have the strength to step into another's weight and help carry it. Becoming a source of strength, substance, and life-giving encouragement demands that you are willing to step into the gap that exists for others and be a backstop for them, when they can't be one for themselves. Fellas, what does that look like?

- The way you communicate

- The way you support

- Sharing your stories of pain and victory

- Leveling your pride by overcoming fear and insecurity

- Thriving as a servant

The sum of my pain, shame, and failures pale in comparison to the eternal strength that is building in me. Nearly half of my life was spent in the valley, while there were mountain tops. Tops that I struggled to enjoy because I did not have eternal strength. Development of eternal strength through surrender gave me perspective. Strength does not have to be prideful. It was a rock solid understanding that there is nothing wrong with me, and I am not defective. In the rooms of recovery this is called becoming *right sized*. Joseph Campbell offers this explanation for the Spiritual Hero,

> The Spiritual Hero has learned or found a mode for experiencing the supernormal range of human spiritual life and come back to communicate it. It's a cycle, a going and return, that the hero cycle represents.

By no means am I a spiritual authority or miracle worker. Jesus Christ has that distinction. Through my Hero's Journey, I have been inspired through much pain, suffering, grace and mercy to go on that journey and come back to share the strength, substance, and life-giving encouragement the source of all life has given me. In 2007, I was part of a dynamic Bible study group that included more than 50 people. We met each week for 12 weeks. God was seemingly present every meeting. I was prophesied over, and in that moment with other believers and His spirit present, God called the Oak Tree into being.

One of the members declared that I was strong like an oak tree. A few weeks later, a Pentecostal pastor visited us and invited people to stay and learn how to speak in tongues.

*Suddenly a sound like the blowing of a violent wind came from heaven and filled the whole house where they were sitting. They saw what seemed to be tongues of fire that separated and came to rest on each of them. All of them were filled with the Holy Spirit and began to speak in other tongues as the Spirit enabled them.*
*—Acts 2:2-4*

Before you question this practice, hear the rest of the story. That night, I was baptized in the Holy Spirit's fire. The spirit laid upon me, and as a result I made two powerful decisions that have come to define my strength on this Hero's Journey.

When I got home to my apartment complex, I took my dog to the park where we always walked. It was one that I always prayed in; many times danced and praised God's name; and sometimes, wrestled with Him. On this night, God called me to do more. There was a group of at least a dozen teenagers playing and running around in the park. As I entered the park, I asked God, "Where do we go from here?"

Without hesitation, my gaze turned to the group of kids. The Holy Spirit prompted me to go tell them about Jesus Christ. My first thought was "No" and I walked the other way. After walking some 50 feet, I turned and reversed course, now walking toward the kids. I asked if I could talk to them for a few minutes, and they all proceeded to sit down. I told them the story of what had happened to me that night. They listened intently. It seemed like they were hanging on every word I said as I explained that the spirit of Jesus had come upon me and how important a personal relationship with Him is. I stressed that a relationship with Jesus would change their lives in ways they could not imagine, and that Jesus Christ loved them. It was like a classroom in the park with engaged students and an inspired teacher.

If I had any doubts about God's best for me that night, and where He was leading me, that night was a starting point. An *Oak Tree Source* develops the courage and confidence every day to heed the call of significance. Less than two years later, I was applying to go to college to finish my degree and become a teacher and football coach, full-time. I just finished year seven teaching and now am a Head JV Coach and QB Coach.

God's personal call on my life is in full motion and gaining momentum every day when I give Him the credit. When God moves, there is no stopping what He has planned for your life. When you know you are being led by the Holy Spirit, the impossible becomes possible. Heaven descends upon earth just as Jesus decreed in the Lord's prayer "on earth as it is in Heaven." God uses those who are obedient and intent on giving Him the credit. God only operates with substance. Heeding the call....

From the time I was eleven, I had been seeing a psychologist off and on. He was a man I respected greatly for his insight and compassion. I told him about my experience from the speaking in tongues session. He explained it as being part of a large crowd and getting caught up in the energy of the crowd. He asked me other questions regarding being healed emotionally or having a new thought process, and I could not point to one specific thing.

I sensed his skepticism, but this I knew: unequivocally, my experience that was seeded by the Bible study group was the most important experience of my life. At the end of our session that day, my psychologist gave me an ultimatum. Accept the experience for what it was, a crowd driven energy phenomenon, or our times meeting together would be over.

I agonized on the decision for a couple of days. This man had been a mentor and a source of wisdom for me for years and he was forcing me to choose: him or my faith in Jesus Christ.

I could not deny the spirit of the living God was in me that night when I spoke in tongues and when the teens gathered around me. Thus, the choice became an easy one: break with my psychologist. A new strength, a new freedom was born that night in the park and the decision to part ways with my past. The hand of God was on me and has been near me since. I pray the prayer of Jabez every day that includes:

*Asking God to bless me today;*
*Expanding my territory;*
*Having His hand on me;*
*Keeping me from evil;*
*Causing no pain; and*
*Fighting my battles with and for me.*

An *Oak Tree Source* is not afraid to go first, no matter how ill equipped that person thinks he or she is. The *Oak Tree Source* understands the source of all life is behind him or her and draws strength from it.

> The freedom to make decisions based on identity and the strength that comes with it instead of passively swaying with the tide of the crowd has become a hallmark in my journey in becoming an *Oak Tree Source*. The ability to recall, resolve, and restore my identity is purposefully satisfying on levels I did not think possible. Another cornerstone is experiencing the purposeful satisfaction that comes with being a source of strength, substance, and life-giving encouragement.

My quest for knowledge was at full throttle. As I learned more and more about myself, how I can best serve this world, best encourage and love others, and experience purposeful satisfaction, I came across the Clifton Strength Finder. The strength finder is designed to help individuals identify their strengths so they can maximize their abilities, talents, and skills in their chosen endeavors. I took the strength finder analysis and found the results can shed light and support my journey to strengthening myself in the Lord.

One of the hashtags I use on my social media platforms is #relationalleadership. My strength finder profile identified my leadership style as *Relationship Building*. Leaders with relationship building traits are the essential glue that holds a team together. It's their strength. Without a relationship building leader on a team, a team usually isn't a team, but merely a composite of individuals. Relationship building leaders create groups and organizations that are much greater than the sum of their parts.

**The most vital asset to authentic strength is integrity.**

As a source of strength, substance, and life-giving encouragement, an *Oak Tree Source* draws its nourishment from the living—the giving water that relationships generates. The mission becomes to be the relational starting point for people so they can realize greater potential within themselves, become "a part of" so that they can experience something greater than themselves.

Being a source of strength, substance, and life-giving encouragement is the glue, the bond, which can hold a team, a culture, a movement, together long after the shine of team building wears off and the challenges of significance, healing, and production are front and center each day.

The parallels between a source (starting point) of strength, substance, and life-giving encouragement and learning, positivity, belief, individualization, and the ability to help create context for your family, friends, colleagues, and teams are uncanny. I often tell people that I have lived two lives, the one filled with shame, pain, pride, and failure and the one I am living now in freedom and victory as one of Kafele's seed spreaders.

The most vital asset to authentic strength is integrity. Integrity means that my thoughts, emotions, beliefs are in alignment with my actions and words. Acting from my strengths enables me every day to pour out strength, love, and encouragement because I am not weighed down by the pushing and pulling of a personal battle for my life. Yet, I'm able to carry weight and the burden of others because I am an *Oak Tree Source.*

> *It is curious that physical courage should be so common in the world and moral courage so rare.* —Mark Twain

# coach gus' insights

Your most vital asset to authentic strength is integrity. Your thoughts, emotions, and beliefs are in alignment with your actions and words. When you act from your strengths, you become stronger personally and professionally.

# 3 Substance

Depth and substance:

The two most exquisite qualities . . .

Be it in a poem or a person.

—Sanober Khan, poet and author

# chapter ten

# Are You Ready to Serve?

*I had to be willing to challenge all my beliefs as they pertained to manhood.*

I posed a question to myself: *How could I become meaningful or important to my family and my students if I didn't choose a new path?* It all started with self-reflection . . . my willingness to investigate the mirror of my life. What had it evolved into? And I didn't want the reflection I saw to be part of me any longer.

Personal substance is such an encompassing concept. The stuff that you and I are made of is complex. When you encounter people of substance, there is an undeniable presence that they carry themselves with. Substance and presence are synonymous with living a well-integrated life. Substance can be defined by the tangible matter that creates a solid presence, for example, the physical properties found in nature, architecture of physical structures, and the human body. There is so much more that explains substance when it comes to human beings.

The essentials of life as described by Abraham Maslow in his hierarchy of needs begins at the foundation with "physiological needs" being met: air to breathe, water to drink, food to eat and shelter. Maslow's hierarchy ends with "self-actualization," which states, *the desire to become the best you can be.*

What does that mean for men in today's culture? There must be a shift in the way men think of themselves, their roles, and their identity. Where are you in your thinking?

To become self-actualized, reliance on physical strength, male dominance, and traditional positions in the hierarchy must be reconsidered. To create substance, the essentials for life, the significance you crave, you need to look at how pride affects your provider role, your protector role, and your machismo. What are you willing to lose to gain more than you could have imagined?

For me, I had to be willing to lose the narratives that plagued me for so long in my marriage:

*I'm not enough.*
*I'm not 6'4" or think like Carrie.*
*I'm not respected for what I do.*
*I must fight for my standing in our marriage lest I'll be forgotten.*

It was a lot ... and I mean A LOT, to let these narratives disappear.

Creating substance—that meaningfulness in life takes courage and strength. It takes deconstructing the way you have operated to reconstruct your thoughts, beliefs, and actions so that your presence is filled with substance like an oak tree. Imagine your temporal body filled with

> strength and substance. Your presence would look and
> feel like an oak tree, deeply rooted in the source, reaching
> far and wide with purpose and beauty.

For me, as I sat under the Tree of Life in New Orleans in
2018, I was engulfed by its presence, its far reaching branches
and enormous root system ... stunning in its magnitude. Later,
when I saw the picture that John
Brooks had taken of me sitting
under the tree, it became so clear

**What are you willing to
lose to gain more than
you could have imagined?**

to me why God has prophesied over me, mentioning the oak
tree. John is my closest friend and has always helped me see the
substance of life.

Men, I hope that all of you have a friend like John Brooks,
who tells you the truth about yourself, is unequivocally reliable,
and cares about the betterment of your life by sharing wisdom
and experience that comes from becoming a source of strength
and substance. This is why John's nickname is "Yoda."

When I envision being a source of strength, substance, and
life-giving encouragement, the oak tree becomes the perfect
symbolism. To grow your presence with depth and breadth,
you need to look at examples of what it looks like and how you
can grow deeper and wider. What is it about the presence—
appearance, demeanor—of someone or something that can be
attractive or even captivating? Is it the physical appearance ...
features of someone or something? You know presence when
you feel it. You know presence when you see it, but that's only
part of the story.

Living in Colorado, I am in the presence of majestic physical
geography that lures tens of thousands to Colorado to establish

residence and to enjoy the grandeur of the Rocky Mountains. There is so much to be said for the rejuvenating effects of hiking Mount Princeton or climbing the stairs among the red rocks in Red Rocks Park. I can think of so many places at home and abroad that would light up your spirit with their beauty and majesty.

What about people who have an undeniable presence? Is it their physical stature or their beauty? Maybe it's their physical strength? Or their radiating perfect smile? These are undeniable visual attributes that stand out. I have walked a few steps behind Michael Jordan trying to catch his attention; ran to the feet of John Elway for an autograph; and have been huddled around Jack Nicklaus to shake his hand. Michael Jordan and John Elway had undeniable physical attributes that made them stand out, and yet it was Jack Nicklaus who had a warmth about him that stood out even more. His smile was genuine; his being was

**Treat people as human beings.** inviting. Jack Nicklaus also seemed to be more available mentally and emotionally than either Michael Jordan or John Elway in those moments when I was in their presence.

Did circumstances have something to do with these incredible and talented men being open or not? No doubt about it. Did I project onto them what I believed about who they were? It is very likely. *You are in the presence of greatness* … we have all heard this phrase. Yet are you really?

These three sports figures have achieved greatness in their respective professions time and time again. They have been lauded by the media, by their fans, by various halls of fame, and certainly in their bank accounts.

*Does this equate to their having an inviting and available presence that connects to others? No, not at all.*

*Does it mean they will be automatically gracious and humble because of all the adoration they receive? No, not at all.*

Denny Dillard is a dear friend who was on the Los Angeles Police Force in the late 1980s and early '90s when gang violence was spiking, and racial tension was high. I had the extreme good fortune of doing some self-defense training with him. He consistently talked about having a *command presence*—a phrase unfamiliar to me. In law enforcement, the military, and self-defense worlds, it is crucial to establish a command presence.

Perpetrators, enemy combatants or attackers are looking for any sign to take advantage of you. Establishing a command presence not only breeds confidence within you, but it also tells your foes—should they choose to engage you—they are not going to have a walk in the park. Along with learning defense measures, THE MOST IMPORTANT piece of wisdom Denny imparted to me was to treat people as human beings. Even though he wore the shield, and there was a certain perception of him because of that, he treated those he brought to justice as human beings first, always. Sadly, the United States is currently struggling with racial tension and police brutality.

**Exercising power for the sake of power will never be an answer that endures and sustains life.**

As a man of substance, Denny Dillard stands out. There are too many police officers who abuse the privilege and duty of the shield. As I wrote this chapter in June of 2020, there were protests all over the United States because of law enforcement abuse. These protests scream from the heart of men (and women) who have been treated unjustly—certainly not equal to their fellow man.

These passionate pleas from the heart speak to a core issue in American society. Too often, men, it doesn't matter their race, color, or nationality, are using their power based in ego, such as conquest and dominance. These behaviors do not allow them to see past the intoxication that power unleashes. Much like manufactured strength, exercising power for the sake of power will never be an answer that endures and sustains life.

- Substance sustains you when difficulty and disappointment are front and center.

- Substance drives you to what is pure, loving, and trustworthy. The force of authentic substance pulls us to positive action.

- Substance is like an invisible hand at your back, gently, but authoritatively moving you toward more of the essential stuff that creates authenticity in your presence that is undeniable.

*Authentic presence* and *substance* are woven themes throughout my life as it is today and within the pages of *The Oak Tree Source*. To understand what authentic presence in creating a life of substance means, ask yourself if you operate with the following three described attributes. These distinct attributes —availability, freedom, command—indicate an authentic presence. Each is interconnected.

**AVAILABILITY** is the essential ingredient to an authentic presence. Availability means you don't need anything. You show up with a mental and emotional presence that acts from a place of abundance.

**FREEDOM** appears as an abundant posture that attracts others to your emotional substance because of your life experiences and introspection that resulted in greater freedom.

**COMMAND** surfaces when you are in a secure position: mentally, emotionally, and spiritually. It enables you to be free and available yet have clear emotional boundaries that allow for real warmth and connection without rigidity.

Jesus exemplifies this in his teachings from the Sermon on the Mount using the metaphors of salt and light.

*You are the salt of the earth. But if the salt loses its saltiness, how can it be made salty again? It is no longer good for anything, except to be thrown out and trampled underfoot.*

*You are the light of the world. A town built on a hill cannot be hidden. Neither do people light a lamp and put it under a bowl. Instead, they put it on its stand, and it gives light to everyone in the house. In the same way, let your light shine before others, that they may see your good deeds and glorify your Father in heaven.*

—Matthew 5:13–16

Jesus used the word *salt* comparing it to the enhancement and preservation of food. The salt in the life of a believer in Christ is a life enhancer for others. And *light* reinforces what Jesus said: letting your light shine before others.

Your presence is imperative to affect this world. You can be a starting point for yourself, and be a source of life-giving encouragement, love, and strength. The direction you then take leads to an undeniable substance in the way you live and act. The result? A purpose led satisfaction that is rooted deep in your heart. It is your Oak Tree maturing to full growth.

You now ponder:

Can I be more available?

Can I be freer?

Can I be more in command?

*Can you?*

If you are willing to be a starting point (source) and examine your availability, choose freedom, and carry yourself with command as a result, your presence can illuminate and surround you, and those around you with the substance and strength of an oak tree.

Let them feel your presence, fellas. I had to be willing to challenge all my beliefs as they pertained to manhood. What I was fed, and the corresponding belief that manifested from it, did not serve me well when I was faced with my own short-comings. There is a real fear out there among men that their manhood will be taken away, literally emasculated, if they do not act from the primal and physical self of who they are.

Entering anything less than an authoritarian posture shows weakness and vulnerability.

The scientific definition of emasculation is the removal of the penis and testicles. The metaphorical definition of emasculation is, "depriving a man of his role or identity" … such as: "in his mind, her success emasculated him."

That sentence defined me for the first few years of my marriage. As I stated earlier, in my mind's eye, my wife's successes were emasculating me. It is easy and lazy to dig in with our egos and manliness and operate from here for a lifetime. Yet, there is no denying that love and connection move humanity toward authentic substance over force and physicality. What is even more attractive about creating substantive strength is this:

**Jesus gives us this piercing truth.**

> Your male identity and role as a provider only becomes stronger if you become the starting point, *the source.*

In the Gospel according to John, Jesus gives us this piercing truth, which shows His command in His presence.

> *Jesus went to the Mount of Olives. Early in the morning he came again to the temple. All the people came to him, and he sat down and taught them. The scribes and the Pharisees brought a woman who had been caught in adultery and placing her in the midst they said to him, 'Teacher, this woman has been caught in the act of adultery.'*
>
> *Now in the Law, Moses commanded us to stone such women. 'So, what do you say?' This they said to test him that they might have some charge to bring against him. Jesus bent down and wrote with his finger on the ground. And*

*as they continued to ask him, he stood up and said to them,
'Let him who is without sin among you be the first to throw
a stone at her.' And once more he bent down and wrote on
the ground. But when they heard it, they went away one by
one, beginning with the older ones, and Jesus was left alone
with the woman standing before him. Jesus stood up and said
to her, 'Woman, where are they? Has no one condemned you?'*

*She said, 'No one, Lord.'*

*And Jesus said, 'Neither do I condemn you; go, and from
now on, sin no more.'*

—John 8: 1-11

Jesus shows us three powerful examples of strength and
substance in this story. First, people came to him, and he
was teaching them. There is no better opportunity to exhibit
strength and influence than through teaching, and if you have
substance, people will come to you.

**Meekness is widely associated with weakness.**

Second, Jesus was being questioned
as to Judaic law when he did a peculiar
thing. He bent down and started to write in the dirt. And there
is historical scholarly debate as to why. Yet, I remember so many
times drawing a football play or strategy in the dirt during
capture the flag or a similar game, so we could dictate how the
game was played, and be in a commanding position. I believe
Jesus was in the power position as he pondered his response
to the Pharisees. And when he responded, he pierced the
Pharisees' hearts with a direct and substantive truth that brought
them into a posture that they could not deny this truth.

And third, Jesus did not condemn the woman. He, with such availability, freedom, and command, did not condemn or judge because his objective was to spread seeds of truth and love.

> The term *meekness* is widely associated with weakness. But the term *spiritual meekness* brings a perspective that aligns perfectly for those becoming an Oak Tree Source. Within *The Journey Toward Holiness* by Andrew Murray, he reveals a direct correlation to the substance of meekness and humility:
>
> Men sometimes speak as if humility and meekness would rob us of what is noble, bold, and manlike. O that all would believe that this is the nobility of the kingdom of heaven, that this is the royal spirit that the King of heaven displayed, that this is Godlike, to humble oneself, to become the servant of all!

Murray captures the essence of the Oak Tree Source with eloquence and authority. If you allow the concept of meekness and humility to be the mirror for your beliefs, thoughts, and actions, most likely you are not going to like what reflects.

The mirror analogy is such a powerful concept to allow you to see how you operate and be alerted to those pressure points or pain points that need your attention. Living a life of substance takes the Refiner's Fire that I wrote of in the previous chapter. Refining must be illuminated by those people, places, and things that give rise to your impurities so that your substance becomes essential.

The mirror does this. There is no better mirror than those that are closest to you. Those that see you the most are the ones that mirror for you the affirmation of your thoughts, behaviors, and actions or the condemnation and judgment you live with.

As a first year teacher at Compassion Road Academy (CRA) in the Denver Public School System, I was shown the mirror every day by my students that first semester. I judged that my authoritative and commanding presence combined with my loving and compassionate nature would be the ingredients needed to succeed with my students. I would lead with authority and follow up with love.

In the first month of school my iPad was stolen. Leading with authority produced a standoff of wills that was never going to create belonging and any type of culture in the classroom. I could not gain consistent buy-in from students on a day-to-day basis. Finally, I yelled out like a child wanting to be removed from a situation because I could not get students to get ready to start our lesson. I seriously questioned whether this was the place for me to teach. When I took the job at CRA, it was another journey defining choice. Upon making the choice, the image that reflected at me was, "You have what it takes!"

On some level, I knew the substance that I was made of would be challenged and made purer by this experience. I was told going into the assignment that I would

**I came to serve.**

be challenged emotionally because the kids were dealing with extraordinary challenges and pressures outside the classroom that sometimes would challenge their teachers, too.

Little did I know how extraordinary some of them were. As I grew, these challenges helped me become more like Jesus. After that first semester, I realized that I was not going to "will" or "coach" my way into the hearts of these young people. Leading with love and connection was the only way to connect with them. In the process, I got to love myself on a deeper level because I had been through some of the things the kids had. Instead of crying out like a child or trying to exert my will over the kids, I started to walk shoulder to shoulder with them.

I was connecting on the heart level first. The job became very gratifying and much of what I entered teaching to do. I came to serve. The greatest gauge of substance building in your life comes when you understand the condition of your heart as it relates to your circumstances and outcomes. When you look into that mirror with the eyes of your heart and see humanity —how you can help, how you can serve, how you can love first —the pure substance of who you are meant to be is shining through.

This attitude, no matter how difficult the day and no matter how undisciplined the students, continued to pervade my thoughts and actions. My aha surfaced: The intersection where trials and hardships meet grace can be so rewarding. I continued to look to serve first. This transformed into buying my classes' breakfast at the local food truck sometimes during our morning breaks or when special occasions surfaced during class, such as students completing a curricular objective. I realized that some students may not have eaten breakfast or eaten at all recently. Food is such a powerful incentivizer but so is education.

The power of education cannot be understated. Education comes in so many forms. While teachers get paid to teach curriculum, advance kids toward mastery of content, teaching encompasses the person. The urgency with which this was shown to me at CRA was so beneficial. At the district level, the powers that be watch the bottom line: Are GPAs increasing?

Are more students graduating? Rightfully so, the objective of schools is quantitative in its data measurements. Yet, as a first-year school teacher touching hearts, I led the charge to measure the qualitative data.

The quality of the incremental steps I took to engage students in their classes and overall well-being was real, along with building trust and social capital to create a safe place for students to feel loved every day. I sat in many meetings where quantitative data flashed across the projector, was colored coded and divided into tiers so that we teachers could see which color we fell under and where we needed to grow. Analytics are meaningful. They inform you as to trends and patterns that can uncover inefficiencies and move you toward more useful ways of operating.

I remember the first in-class evaluation I received from one of the district's classroom evaluators. Initially nervous, the class did not seem to run smoothly or engage as I would have liked. For the assignment, we were rewriting our definition of social justice after gathering research and background. As students were working, I was rushing around giving feedback. I loved the shared responsibility the students took to come up with a meaningful definition of the topic. It was a productive class.

In the moment, I could not have cared less about my quantitative evaluation. The substance that was produced that day in class was validated in my evaluation. As a first time teacher, in a hard to serve setting, I received sixes in most categories—a rating of six means you are highly effective, a rating of seven is distinguished. As I drove home that night, satisfaction washed over me. I was doing exactly what I was made to do: Teach and coach, act as a source of strength, substance, and life-giving encouragement.

I will never forget a Friday in April when gang members came to our school ready to fight some of our students as school was letting out. The root word for substance is to "stand firm," "be under," or "be present." I stood firm between our students and gang members as they started to come across the street, but they hesitated. There was no confrontation. I would like to think that my physical presence was the deterrent that day.

*The greatest ability is dependability.*   —Bob Jones

# coach gus' insights

Building substance as an individual leads to self-efficacy that produces a solid and dependable presence. Quite possibly, the greatest compliment a person can receive is, "I can depend on you."

I take such great pride in being dependable. This is an essential quality of becoming an Oak Tree Source.

# chapter eleven

# Transcending Fears and Shortcomings

*Substance gives you an anchor to come back to
when people, places, and things let you down.*

Before Carrie and I were married, she gave me a birthday card. Inside the card was a quote from John Wayne:

*If you got them by the balls,
their hearts and minds will follow.*

This is such a poignant quote that epitomizes a way of operating for men for centuries. There is something substantive to a masculinity that is powerful, rugged, and relentless in its exhibition of strength. From generation to generation, most men believe this is how we are supposed to act as men. Do you?

Conquering those places inside that make you feel weak and blocking out those thoughts and actions that do not exhibit maximum strength and power is the manly thing to do. With this mindset comes an inability or unwillingness to show emotion. Eventually emotions come out through your words and actions.

For many men, they are expressed in sarcasm, anger, dominance, or bullying. After those expressions, whining or thoughts of inadequacy emerge. Inadequacy is a corrosive thread that steals your substance and your strength. Inadequacy happens when you compare yourself to others. If you compare your insides to others' outsides, you will never measure up.

Have you ever thought about the massive amount of advertising targeted toward men? Why is there so much advertising **My greatest fear** referencing magic pills that will make men **is having regrets.** bigger and stronger, or ones that make the penis bigger or an erection last longer? In my work, I've been able to sum up the answer in just a few words: because inadequacy is an epidemic in men today.

> Do you compare yourself on the outside, and then not want to do the work on the inside that will give you authentic strength? Strength can develop essential substance that transcends your fears and shortcomings. Think about it. When you transcend your fears and shortcomings, what happens? You transform your life. When you don't compare yourself to every Tom, Dick, and Harry you come across, your life becomes center stage. Men, you must be ready to be who you were meant to be. You were meant to live a life that stands for something, a life that is significant. In the end you can be purposefully satisfied with yourself.

My greatest fear is having regrets. In the first quarter of my life there were choices and behaviors that I regret. Firmly entrenched in the second quarter of life, I refuse to have regrets. There is a line from the movie *We Bought a Zoo* starring Matt

Damon, where he is revealing to his kids about the first time he saw their mother and how he had approached her. "I needed 15 seconds of insane courage to speak to her."

Think about the insightful statement. My take is that if we can live by this motto we will never have regrets—*you will have no regrets.* If you lead with your heart and mind, the substance of who you are shines through. And your thoughts, behaviors, actions, and choices take on meaning and significance.

On the road to creating substance, there have been times when I have the burn, the desire to cut loose my male dominance and put the scoreboard up so I can tell the world, "Don't you know who I am? Don't you know what I've accomplished?" By erecting the scoreboard, I can measure myself against others in my profession, other men I see doing great things and making a difference. Or I want to take my rightful place as the bread-winner in our household. *Is that some-thing you've engaged in?*

**Male dominance fails when we crash into and run over others.**

This classic expression of masculinity leads to a narrow perspective that men settle for. Not only can you let your masculinity exude strength and power in the traditional sense, but you can also create the essential stuff: connection, belonging, respect, influence, and legacy. There needs to be a critical balance of masculine and feminine strength.

I know … I know … there will be men who read this and think I'm crazy. Ask yourself this question, fellas … when does your significant other give you the "soul eyes" that stare love right through you? When you hunt or conquer a new job, a difficult project? Sure … what about when you show her the shape of your heart, your vulnerability? My guess is you know the answer to that question. This is substance, fellas!

Male dominance fails when we crash into and run over others. My first year in recovery, I was asked to play softball with the AA club I attended. I was happy to be a part of the team and show off my skills as a ball player, thinking this would help me gain acceptance. The team asked me to come and practice softball. I thought they were crazy. I said, "I don't have to practice softball. Don't they know who I am?" *I am the drunk who blew his chance to play big league ball. And I'm so good, I don't need to practice.*

With this attitude, I missed the entire point of why the team was practicing. They weren't practicing to strictly focus on playing ball. They were practicing so they could create connection and belonging. This was something that I sorely missed and yearned for. I started to show up for practice and connected with the team and made some friends for life. And the bonus … I met the love of my life.

My next step … I started to create the essential stuff (substance) that life is made of. You do this by:

- Finding the critical balance in your life;

- Widening your perspective of male dominance; and

- Creating connection and belonging out of a substantive perspective and balance.

In coed softball, there is a "male dominance" rule that states if a female has a chance to catch or field a ball, a male cannot step in to make the play for her. If he does, the hitter is automatically awarded first base. Whoa, this was a "new rule" for me to grasp and practice. I wanted to win so badly that I would run down shallow fly balls that our female second baseman could have made the play on. I was called for male dominance on more than a few occasions, and even ran physically into her a couple of times in my desire to show off how good I was.

The reality is that dominating as a male—for the sake of dominating—will put you in collision with others on a constant basis, and it becomes tiring. In recovery softball, there are players with varying skill levels. This was frustrating for me as an ultra-competitor. I thought I had to carry the team and be the perfect player … ALL THE TIME. Have you ever felt like you have had to carry the entire load . . . in your profession, your marriage, your family of origin?

The light bulb turned on. What I realized on the field was: I cannot always be perfect, but I can set the tone in how I compete. And now I can coach and teach the girls and the guys on how to be better ball players and set the tone so they can be more successful. This worked. I could compete at the level I wanted to, and love everyone around me through coaching and teaching, most importantly exhorting and encouraging the team to be greater!

The culmination of my time playing recovery softball happened during our end of year tournament in 2008. I proposed to Carrie earlier in the week and won the first ever Most Valuable Player award in the league. Not for my physical skills as a player … as a team member who finally got the power of balance and supported the team. The entire league celebrated with us, a proposal and MVP. The picture of me holding Carrie in one arm and the MVP trophy in the other was the perfect embodiment of connecting with balance and perspective.

If "the win" is your driver, at some point you are going to run into a ceiling if you continue to dominate without balance and perspective. When you operate from these principles, everything about your mind, body, and soul change. You are not in conflict. You don't fight for or against the things you want and the things you are trying to let go of.

Before Carrie and I started dating, I had dated many women looking for "The One." On a couple of occasions, my mind told me that I had found her. I was ready to take the leap into a committed relationship, and I became a smotherer. As it turned out, neither woman was ready or willing to take that leap with me. In retrospect, I overwhelmed them with my desires and needs, which is not the formula for creating a lasting relationship.

During this time, I sought the counsel of Heather and Carrie. Heather is a dear friend and Carrie's best friend. Our softball team was a very close group. We had many get togethers, and many times Heather and Carrie and I talked about life, and everything in my dating life. Not realizing it at the time, but Carrie and I were getting to know each other on a substantive level, which would ultimately set the foundation for our future together. I confided in both girls about the struggles and the disappointments of my previous relationships.

Heather and Carrie saw ME, and my vulnerabilities. I began to work at expressing myself in an authentic way that resonated. I wasn't trying to impress or be something I was not. I felt safe with both girls. There is no doubt that this helped with my level of vulnerability. These conversations helped me understand that what I desired and the intention that I focused on them could be reflected and confirmed. It was a huge step for me.

Heather and Carrie were further down the road of experience with clean living and sober thought, yet all three of our desires to connect authentically and be loved by our higher power was the common ground that we became closer through. Fourteen years later, as Carrie and I enter our twelfth year of marriage, I am moved to tears as I write this. The essential substance that our marriage is made of started with those conversations. I firmly believe everyone is on a collision course with the essential substance they are becoming.

> God was pouring out His love and grace, and I needed to trust Him.

Years ago, my good friend Steve Salinas, the managing broker at the Keller Williams Realty office I worked at in the late 1990s, gave me a piece of advice that was prophetic at the time, and still is today. We were talking about relationships, and he told me, "The woman you will be with is being molded right now so that she will be ready for you." I would not have characterized myself as ready for marriage to Carrie. And I thought she was "out of my league" anyway. What I could not see in myself—the perceived readiness or worthiness—God was pouring out His love and grace, and I needed to trust Him. I'm so glad I did. This one decision to trust that, in the white hot fire, God would protect me and continue to push the impurities out of me and that my essential substance would remain—divine substance.

These experiences have led me to a leadership style that resembles transformational leadership. Through my own transformation, a set of ideals, an inspirational countenance, and individual care and concern for others has emerged that drives me every day. The transformational leadership model is led by the ability to inspire, create intellectual buy -in, and live with integrity so that others follow and make those on the team known individually so that they can work to their highest and best capacity. Inspiration is part of my natural makeup, evidenced by the exhorting of teammates and coaches during that 1990 State Championship Run at Cherry Creek High School. It took me two decades to add substance to my leadership style.

Experience is invaluable, yet the times where I took risks and jumped into the journey where there was a game being played that I did not even know about—God's game—is where my explosive growth happened. Does growth **Changed lives** *always* happen in an explosive manner? If it **change lives.** did, I don't know that we as humans could handle it mentally, emotionally, physically, and spiritually. I am incredibly grateful for the Refiner's Fire that burned the impurities out of me and has led me to live a life with the anchors of honesty, steadfastness, and truth.

Living with these anchors does not reach a destination. Living out of the protection of the Refiner's Fire means you can live with abandon. It does not mean you will be without trials and challenges. The trials and challenges take on new meaning, which becomes the force through which the Holy Spirit leads us … leads you. You become more like Jesus.

What would the worth be in discarding the attitudes and beliefs that do not serve us without changing, seeing things with more clarity, and being someone worth following? This transformation into adding substance to your life brings with it influence. *Changed lives change lives.* It is a powerful statement that all men should be striving for each day.

By leading through a framework of change, your influence can be more substantive and transformational. The idea of change is attractive to people, especially when it is positive change. Have you seen changes in people's habits and attitudes that reflect negative traits? As a result, others question and may shy away if they see negative habits and attitudes leading to unhealthy behaviors and actions. Many condemn others who are acting in an unhealthy manner.

If you are a parent, you understand positive change in a profound way. When your children go through all their firsts: words, crawling, walking, riding a bike, etc., watching this transformation not only creates substance for the child ... parents' lives are enriched dramatically. Teachers and coaches get to see these transformations in incredibly substantive ways ... our lives are enriched and deepened dramatically as well.

Taking a team from the beginning of a semester or season to the culmination with every practice, skill-building drills, team scrimmages, learning objectives, cumulative assessment and games is joy personified for a coach. The awe inspiring change that happens through these experiences is the stuff that a "calling" is made of. These types of change can happen all the time. It does not need to be in the nursery, classroom, or field of play exclusively.

You can become an oak tree with deep roots in a boardroom, corner office, workshop, cubicle, and every area of your life. You have the ability to adapt, overcome, and be brave enough to keep changing. Leading with integrity will ensure that you are a source of substance, strength, and life-giving encouragement. Respect and trust are built on the last statement. If you lead with integrity, the positive changes that happen within you are something to be emulated.

There is a holiness that you project when you have been changed; when you lead with integrity; when you become a starting point (source) for others; and when you give the best of yourself consistently.

I want people to look at me and feel my presence with a peculiar look on their faces. Not only do they feel a depth and weight to the way I carry myself, but they see the loving presence of God, his substance pouring out of me. The presence of God in someone is not a regular occurrence. It is unique, rare, or exceptional. The motivation for *The Oak Tree Source* was centered around an unusual life experience and transformation that God said needed to be shared with other men.

For me, my transformation and bridging with God was … well, peculiar. In its pure form it is extraordinary. When you feel it … accept it. Some other synonyms for "peculiar" also include strange, odd, unusual, abnormal, and freaky. What people don't understand, they put in a category or compartment that fits a narrow perspective. An understanding for peculiar that is divergent from holiness and glory emerges. Being filled with glory and holiness sets you apart from the world. By no means does it make anyone special, but it does create substance in your soul and presence that is undeniably peculiar to the world.

If living a substantive life puts up a mirror for society to see that life can be much more meaningfully lived, and the invitation to do so is ever present, becoming Kafele takes on significant importance in this day and age. Living a life that is in search of substance sustains and protects you when you are inevitably faced with your limitations. Substance gives you an anchor to come back to when people, places, and things let you down.

*Let them feel the weight of who you are, then let them deal with it.* —John Eldredge

# coach gus' insights

Acorn to grow: the worth of a more substantive life is beyond measure. Substance is the essential and most important stuff you are made of. It takes hard work, discovery, and patience to fill yourself with it.

# 4 Critical Spirit and Condemnation

Take my yoke upon you and learn from me, for I am gentle and humble in heart, and you will find rest for your souls. For my yoke is easy and my burden is light.

—Matthew 11:29-30

chapter twelve

# Your Critical Spirit

*When the critical lens seeps into your view of humanity
and relationships, condemnation is not far behind.*

The title of this chapter and the Mathew 11:29-30 verse
that opens Part 4 are polar opposites. So, is living a life
of condemnation while striving to live in the light and hope
of Jesus Christ even possible? Left to your own thoughts and
ways of making sense of and acting in this world, you are
susceptible to being hypercritical and condemning of yourself
and others. Maybe in your professional life you are responsible
for pouring over data ... evaluating, analyzing, and synthesiz-
ing through a critical lens. Have you ever critically evaluated
the situation in the nation to a degree that divides you every
minute of the day?

There is a school of thought in the West that suggests that
you must be obsessed with success if you are to reach the lofty
goals you set. It encourages you to amass accolades and riches in
your professional domain. As a business owner, you may wonder:
Why don't my employees have the drive that I do to make this
company the best?

What happens when this critical drive bleeds into your relationships? You may bring the critical lens home ... questioning

**The critical spirit leads to unrealistic expectations.** why your spouse, partner, or child is doing whatever "it is" in that particular way? When the critical lens seeps into your view of humanity and relationships, condemnation is not far behind. The critical spirit leads to unrealistic expectations and robs those around you of their dignity.

In American culture, we are assertive and obsessed with climbing to the top. This *can do* spirit has made the United States a country that is envied around the world. Along with that "can do" spirit comes a critical thought process that calls for the work to be better, to be refined, and to be the best. In making something the best you can, you analyze, evaluate, and interpret everything about the work. It's your critical eye, focusing on the details, breaking down all possible outcomes, teaching an objective or technique tirelessly to help an endeavor be the best it can be. It seems to be a prerequisite for success.

Successful people do not let the details escape them. They prepare for every possible outcome. As a high school teacher,

**When organizations capture a symmetry between the "can do" and "critical" spirit, an authentic culture can emerge.** I constantly challenge my students to think through a critical lens. The more analytical they can be in absorbing variables and connecting those variables to the objective or outcome, the more thorough and satisfying their work will be. These situations lend to constructive criticism that elevates the entire classroom. When organizations capture a symmetry between the "can do" and "critical" spirit, an authentic culture can emerge. The best organizational cultures also have a spirit of "love" and "belonging" woven into the can do and critical spirit.

As a football coach who aspires to coach at the highest level of football, I have seen the level of critical detail that goes into planning and preparation. NFL head coaches are famously known for sleeping at the team facility during the week so they can work 18-hour days and fall onto the couch for a few hours of rest and fall off the couch to get back to their desk and start another day. Often, all the preparation that goes into an NFL game is used to get a "half a man" advantage in the run game, or that specific passing concept or two that the play caller sets up to call it in a crucial part of the game. Critical detail comes down to the smallest piece of an endeavor or project, which in many cases separates the best from the good.

The critical spirit manifests itself in me when I focus too much on my needs in my relationships, which leads me to setting unrealistic expectations of the people I love the most. This cycle leads me to feelings of condemnation—not only for those around me, but for myself. My safety mechanisms around withdrawing from those close to me and pain shopping are magnified through my critical lens.

*Pain shopping* is when your thoughts and spirits focus on finding things in people and places that agree with the condemning narrative you tell yourself. The result is you stay in a self-righteous cycle. Anything that you see or hear that agrees

**When it happens, you know it. Others know it.**

with the narrative you want to tell yourself leaves you trapped, and often you may be oblivious to these traps.

In my work, I present and speak every day. My lesson plan is created for each day. Imagine a room full of high schoolers listening intently and sensing that something is missed, or not clear. Kids know it right away. There is not a worse feeling than when you miss something in an activity, or you miss something in directions or presentations. When it happens, you know it. Others know it.

> If you want to expose yourself and feel naked in front of a large group of people, *don't prepare well.*

> If you want to have the exhilaration of connection and significance, *be well prepared.*

My time as a student teacher became an exercise in preparation and detail. At times, it was critical and condemning. And, many times, it was exhilarating.

What I did not know in content preparation was that I was expected to be the subject matter expert. The only way to become the subject matter expert is to know the content. As part of teaching preparation, you take a content knowledge exam in the area you will be teaching. The social studies content that I was to be an expert in is quite sweeping … all-encompassing actually.

Teaching a specific subject takes in-depth knowledge to become a subject matter expert. Knowledge building takes time and in student teaching, time is lived at light speed. To be prepared to present content, a teacher must anticipate questions that will arise, and understand the breadth and depth of the content so that he or she is not answering a question incorrectly that could steer a student down the wrong path of learning.

For me, I spent hours per night reading content, watching videos that the class would watch, reading articles so our discussions would be substantive, and I could guide the discussions beyond what the articles said. The critical eyes and ears of 30 students and my mentor teacher intently focused on my every word and action was a Refiner's Fire that drove me to condemnation.

I am a person who has suffered from approval seeking and unworthiness, and as a result, I have pain shopped to validate my fears. When I saw a look of disapproval or feedback that was critical, distress signals were created internally. The more the work became demanding and the performance standard I set for myself started to tighten, the distress signals bellowed louder. My internal narrative started like this:

*You don't have what it takes.*
*Why did you change careers to do this?*
*You are such a fool to think you can succeed.*
*I'm not as good as _____.*

These statements led to resentment of myself, yet I directed my frustrations toward my colleagues in the department that I worked in. Eventually, time started to slow down as the semester wore on. And confidence began to build as I developed a curriculum that was engaging and challenging for the students using technology and blogging to express themselves. My final project for student teaching was a 12-lesson unit that would be sent to the Colorado Department of Education and critiqued by my mentor teacher.

At last, the Department of Education granted approval of my lesson unit and my mentor teacher applauded me for use of technology and the ability to outline an effective collaborative platform for students to work in. I was well on my way to becoming a quality teacher.

That spring there was an opening in the social studies department. I interviewed but did not get the job. My student teaching experience allowed me to become immersed in the profession of teaching, yet, even more essential, the experience showed me how to be a more substantive individual. It was a significant step for me.

I got to see the high school experience from a mature perspective. I am reminded of the question I've heard before: "What advice would you give your younger self, knowing what you know now?" I was incredibly fortunate to get a "do over" in life.

As a middle schooler, I was introduced to pornography for the first time. It was a VHS tape of a movie that was much more interesting than any movie I had ever seen. I found times to watch it when my mom and dad were not around. I do not remember how I came into possession of the tape. I do know that it opened a whole new world of sensory stimulation and preoccupation of my mind. This preoccupation would last decades before the pain to keep on with it was greater than the pain of stopping.

Pornography gave me a way to settle for condemning, isolating, and perpetuating shame with the disguise of pleasure. My nature is to be in relationships with others—connecting, sharing, and creating belonging. When it came to girls that

I was attracted to, I had trouble connecting. I felt I had to be something I wasn't, and I put girls and women on a pedestal to be worshipped.

I had wonderful friendships with girls as a kid, even as an adult. When it came to taking the next step into dating or intimacy, frustration set in. It was easier for me to be intimate with alcohol and pornography than a woman. I settled for self-centered fear, and the comfort of my shame before risking letting people know who I was. The pleasure that came with watching porn and masturbating pushed me further from the reality I so desperately wanted.

A study from Brigham Young University by KJ Muller reveals the results of craving versus the reward nature of the brains neurotransmitters when they are rewired to crave a behavior rather than natural rewards. When a craving creates isolation, your isolation prevents you from being a source of strength and substance for others.

Natural rewards are the ability to create belonging and con-nection. Natural rewards are what creates intimacy with another so that the relationship has the chance to become meaningful.

Pornography creates an insidious cycle of manufactured pleasure that fools the brain's neurotransmitters with rewards that manifest isolation. When you are isolated, and not con-nected to others, natural rewards, which the brain was made for, have no room to grow.

**Men, it's a fact: Women are objectified with impunity.**

While there are studies like this that support the addiction concerns of pornography, my story included a change in neurotransmitters that kept me locked in what seemed to be a prison. Rather than seek the "natural reward" of connection and intimacy with a woman, I became addicted to the thrill of watching pornography. That thrill grew into other venues to watch pornography and ultimately it became about the thrill of the behavior. I rationalized these behaviors by telling myself, "I wasn't hurting anyone, I could stay in my personal hell and that was okay."

> Men, it's a fact: Women are objectified with impunity. In corporate America and other large organizations, never-ending lawsuits are filed that demonstrate the practice of sexual harassment or sexual abuse. The definition of objectification is not complicated. It is the action of degrading someone to a mere object.

When you flirt with women but you have a wife or significant other, the prevailing thought is: *It is innocent. No harm, no foul.* Or you daydream about being with those women you flirt with. Few understand that these fantasies are dangerous. Fantasy can slip into reality … your words and actions may push the limit of what is respectful.

My challenge to you is: What do your eyes and body language say about your thoughts? It does not take much discernment to understand our thoughts when we are objectifying women. When you are preoccupied with your desires, or validation, you become distracted. Maybe you start to find fault in your wife, the little things you think she should be doing. You may become a scorekeeper noting, "I have done XYZ … and she hasn't done ABC."

This sounds a lot like the critical spirit and condemnation, doesn't it? The more distracted, critical, and empty you become because you need validation, the more it is likely you will break the marriage covenant or commitment to your spouse. This cycle is passed down to your sons, who see your actions and behaviors and think this is how men treat women.

As fathers of sons, one of your most important jobs is to show them how women should be treated. Men, if you can choose to become a source, and spreader of the seeds of the fruits of the Spirit like Kafele, the result is love, joy, peace, forbearance, kindness, goodness, faithfulness, gentleness, and self-control. Collectively, our sons will see what is true, honest, and steadfast about the marriage relationship and how women should always be treated. If you stay critical and condemning … looking to be filled, you will show them a lack of self-control and self-centeredness that perpetuates harassment and abuse.

At an early age I saw what the critical spirit looked like. My dad used to play football with a group of guys. I was six or seven at the time and went with him every Sunday to watch them play. Every now and again, they let me join in. One morning I got behind the defense and the quarterback threw the ball deep. I caught it and ran it in. Now, the other team might have let me score, but it was a significant happening for me. It may have been the first time that Dad saw the considerable talent in me.

For the next 16 years, he and I created a critical spirit around our love of sports, and we battled because of that critical spirit. I used to wonder: Was I living his dreams or was I living mine? Even though he made my sports experience about him sometimes, sports saved my life! Sports can give you great highs and can also grind you into the ground if you do not have perspective about yourself and the sport(s) you play.

If you are hyperintense, you are being competitive. And if you are competitive, you have a "win at all costs" attitude. Inside the lines, this is where the spirit of competition is at its best. This is where you find out who is willing to do "whatever it takes" to win. Young boys' and girls' characters are molded by these experiences of doing whatever it takes to win and/or achieve. This mindset becomes an obsession where progressing as an athlete means facing tougher competition with even more performance scrutiny. For many years, my father was my number one critic who enabled the existence I led based in shame and condemnation.

When I was a teenager, I chose to pick that critical spirit up and run with it, until it broke me. Part of sports, and better yet, being a male, was comparing myself to other males, and ultimately finding out who the alpha male was or who the best player was. You may have been doing what I did as well.

I loved facing off with the supposed "best players" on opposing teams because I knew I was better than they were, and I would show them. It gave me great satisfaction to win and be the best—the best at anything and everything. From the age of 11 until I was finished playing competitive sports, I sought out the best player from the other team, studied him, and compared my game to his. Not once did I think to myself, "That guy is better than me."

*The emotion that breaks your heart is sometimes the one that heals it.* —Nicholas Sparks

# coach gus' insights

Condemnation can spread quickly in your mind, emotions, and actions. Pain shopping is the best way to stay stuck in the critical spirit and condemning yourself. The emotional weight that is carried by a critical spirit and condemnation of self cannot be understated.

# chapter thirteen

# Slaying the Imposter

*I drank and iced my ankle,*
*pouring gas on my shame and condemnation.*

When my performance did not measure up to my lofty expectations, I pushed harder. I became more critical of my play. The more critical I became, the harder I gripped the bat, and the harder I swung at every pitch. The more anxious I became to succeed and prove my worth, the harder the game was for me. My behavior was coupled with part of my personality based in shame. There was too much noise in my head to play from my natural giftings on a consistent basis. Denny Dillard, my friend and mentor, spoke about the 130 bps threshold for athletes, law enforcement officers, etc., who are engaged in performance, and life or death situations. He said, "130 bps is the optimum space where your mind and body are fully engaged in an activity without anxiety or overexertion."

What does this mean? It means you are in the zone. There is a distinct difference as a hitter when you have a level of calm, yet laser-like focus, as opposed to over anxiousness that leads to scattered focus. With calm and focus, I could swing my bat and hit the ball 400 feet. When anxiety set in, I was like a nervous middle school boy who could not stop tapping his feet, while sitting next to his crush.

My junior year of high school, we played the Mexican Junior National Team who had a one run lead. It was the bottom of the ninth inning with the bases loaded. I came up to the plate expecting to hit a grand slam home run to win the game. I was above that 130 bps zone. The pitcher threw me two straight sliders on the outside corner. On the third pitch, I swung early, trying to pull the ball, and hit a dribbler off the end of the bat right into the glove of the pitcher. He threw to first, and the game was over.

After sulking, I did what I wanted my identity to be. I drank a bunch of beer and thought I was a big leaguer. By the time my senior year of baseball arrived, the identity I had created as a "burn the candle at both ends" guy was widely known. Gone was a big piece of the shine from my junior year as a possible top prospect after hitting three home runs in my first two varsity games. Condemnation was in full effect. I was suspended for our first game for drinking on campus. I was not in great physical or mental shape.

Self-destruction became my constant companion.

The expectations I had for myself were not equal to the preparation and work I put in to realize them. I rolled out of bed and was an All-State player and the 1585th player taken in the 1991 Major League Baseball Amateur draft. Most 18-year-old baseball players would be ecstatic to have those accolades attached to their high school ball playing days. I wasn't. For many years, I considered my playing days a failure. My spirit was so critical and condemning. I often sat in destructive reflection at what could have been. As condemnation continued to grip me, self-destructive behavior went to new levels.

We were in Anaheim, California, playing in the Upper Deck Baseball Classic. Our team was a top 25 team in the country. I was ready to show California that I was one of the best players in the country, not just in Colorado. Our first game started out well. I threw a guy out from right field to save a run from scoring in the first inning. I came to the plate for my first at bat. There was tall metal edging lining the pathway to the batter's box. I stepped into the box, the first pitch came in and the ball looked like a beach ball. My acuity was at peak performance that day.

The second pitch came in. Popping the ball straight up behind the catcher, I moved to get out of the catcher's way. I accidentally stepped on the metal edging and rolled my right ankle. The catcher dropped the ball, so I had another swing, but I could barely put any weight on the ankle as I stepped back in the box. I struck out and hobbled back to the dugout where my ankle had already swelled to the size of an orange.

I missed the rest of that game and three more games over the next three days. I submerged my ankle in a rubber trash can full of ice water over the next few days in hopes of getting back on the field. But there was not going to be a showcase of my talent on the national stage. As my mind did its best to condemn me, I needed relief from that personal hell.

Of course, I had the answer hobbling across the street from the Sheraton Anaheim where we were staying to an AM/PM store. Alcohol was the answer. With a fifth of Southern Comfort and Vodka in my hand, I drank and iced my ankle, pouring gas on my shame and condemnation. My identity was in danger if I could not play ball. My belief was:

*I would not be loved if I didn't play ball.*

*People would not accept me If I did not play ball.*

The shame and condemnation from not playing and drinking heavily turned into anger. On that third night of sitting still, my ankle was feeling better, so I went for a walk around the hotel. As I walked, thoughts of missing out on playing ball, relationships with girls, feeling of failure, culminated in a burst of anger, and I punched through a glass casement that held a fire extinguisher. The fire alarm went off immediately. Unfortunately, or fortunately for the rest of the guests, the fire extinguisher case was in close proximity to the hotel's security office.

**I was a victim of my circumstances, and mad at the world because of the decisions I had made.**

Two security guards quickly grabbed me. My left hand was bleeding. I held my right hand over it to stop the bleeding as the guards questioned me. Ultimately, they called my coach, who came and got me. We'd been together for three years now and he knew me well. We talked until 2 a.m. He was obviously at his wit's end. Our conversation ended with him calling me a *bad apple.*

**I was a bad apple at the ripe age of 18.**

At that point, I was not the leader and inspiration that helped an overmatched football team win a state championship. I was a victim of my circumstances, and mad at the world because of the decisions I had made. Players, my friends, still looked to me, and followed me. A core group on that team drank along side of me. I was a player who expected greatness, but my actions and behaviors spoke to the exact opposite. I was not a good teammate and as tough as it was to hear that night, and as tough as it is to write it now, I was a bad apple at the ripe age of 18.

I could still help the team win though. My ankle was well enough for me to play in our last game of the tournament. I was so happy to be back on the field. I played first base that day instead of right field to minimize how much I ran. Humbled by the events of the week, I just wanted to contribute to the team. I went three for five with two doubles, a single, and three RBIs. We won that game, and I salvaged a little bit of my dignity. Also, I held out the hope that things would get better for me.

One of the defining traits of my life has been the ability to get up after I've been knocked down and finish well. I went on to becoming a first team all-state player later that spring. With many regrets, and a spirit full of criticism, I was ready to put the spring of 1991 behind me and finish my high school sports career on a high note. Unfortunately, there was one more major mishap to come.

Carson City, Nevada, was our next venue. The team stayed in Lake Tahoe where there were beautiful landscapes and lots of casinos. The mistakes I made in the spring had not changed my "burn the candle at both ends" mentality. After a long night at the casinos on the fourth of July, a few teammates and I decided it would be funny to run through some of our other teammates' bedrooms … attacking them with pillows. After some commotion, our coach woke up and came down the stairs from his cabin and said loudly and gruffly, "Get your running shoes on!"

He drove us across the state line to a high school in California. We ran close to seven miles as the sun came up. My coach tells the story to this day. Yet another day that will live in infamy for me, and a lesson for young ball players on what NOT to do.

During my first 31 years of life, I was quite good at being an example of what not to do when it came to decision making, work ethic, plus treating myself and others with respect and honor. I thought there was something wrong with me. There was something missing. I was not smart enough, not handsome enough, and definitely not cool enough. My teeth were not straight, my skin wasn't clear, and I was pigeon-toed. A day didn't go by that I wasn't critical of myself.

American aphorist Mason Cooley was known for his witty aphorisms and summed up my life and the critical spirit incredibly well: "The critical spirit never knows when to stop meddling." Meddling was my way of comparing myself to every guy who had something I wanted or who challenged what I thought I was best at.

My romance with the art of self-destruction continued.

I have always had an acute awareness of what was going on around me. This can be a blessing and a curse. Until I could see myself in a proper perspective, my awareness was on hyperalert most of the time and felt like a curse. My identity came from who I was as a quarterback and right fielder.

After a two year stint at New Mexico Junior College, where I made first team All-Conference my freshman year while hitting .390 with 10 home runs and 50 runs batted in, the Houston Astros did not pick up my draft rights when the season ended. That summer I was out with friends who got into an argument with a group of guys who followed us when we left the bar. I was driving. One car pulled in front of me and stopped. The other car pulled up to the driver's side, boxing us in. I was too drunk to defend myself in the fight that followed.

It was a beautiful summer night in Colorado and our windows were down, which made it easy for fists to come flying in the window. I was hit multiple times, and all I could do was cover up. I don't know how many times I was hit, but enough to break my jaw. Alcohol consumption had put me in another vulnerable and dangerous situation, which had physically harmed me. My jaw was wired shut from June until August.

**Nothing was going to change if nothing changed.**

When I returned to school that fall, I was hopeful that I would capture my strong play from the previous year. I was hopeful that I would get drafted again and sign with a major league baseball team. Nothing was going to change if nothing changed. My behavior was the same as it had always been and that would be my undoing. Not surprisingly, I was kicked off the team after more poor decision making and lack of discipline as a student and ball player.

After the 1993 season, the childhood dream of being a professional athlete was over. The persona that I carried as the "burn the candle at both ends" ball player and night life king was gone. When sports ended for me much earlier than I thought it was going to, there was a void that left me scared and uncertain.

My friends were finishing college and starting to build lives. The void in me felt like a black hole that was pulling me further into nothingness. It became so bad for me that on a few occasions I would be standing in line at a movie or ball game and people bumped into me. Apologizing, it was common for them to say, "I did not even know you were there." These people could have very easily not been looking and innocently bumped into me. But for me, it reinforced my lack of presence and poured more fuel on the fire of shame inside of me.

I was becoming invisible, and this existence felt safe for me. Safety meant not taking risks in relationships, not trying new hobbies or interests, or career pursuits. Any ambition I once had evaporated. I had never seen anything but sports as my career path … my work. I continued to be primarily focused on acceptance, approval, and living fast. Until I was almost 30 years old, I still lived at my mom's house.

It was a time of unhealthy reflection. My identity was a ball player. I did not finish college, and I had not learned an alternative skill or trade to start a career. When what you have **The war of Britt Gusmus still raged inside me.** done is no longer a career option and you have not learned or adapted your natural skill set to find a career to grow in, your options narrow dramatically.

In my twenties, there were brief moments at my miscellaneous jobs that were satisfying. I worked for a good friend's window cleaning company that handled some major projects in the Denver area at the time. We did the initial construction cleanup at Coors Field and a wing of the Broadmoor West addition. I became a receptionist at a national real estate company that had offices in Denver. These were only fill-in jobs. There was nothing that I felt could be a career path opportunity.

The war of Britt Gusmus still raged inside me. My outsides matched the shame and condemnation I lived with. I was overweight, and I scowled quite a bit in critical reflection, which left a line in the middle of my brow that is a fixture on my facial landscape today. Chalk full of pride, I knew that I had more skill and talent than that of a window washer or receptionist. I was living an unfulfilled life.

I was unfulfilled but still clinging to my pride. And then there was my ego. The paradox of my ego—and yours—tells the story of promotion and protection. The ego can help you act from a positive self-image, but it can also act as a protector of your fears, holding you back from your authentic self as it did me. In *Abba's Child*, author Brennan Manning calls the ego protection concept *the imposter*. Imposters practice the art of deception and are frauds—to themselves and to others. They are often educated and accomplished yet live in a lie fueled be self-doubt and a feeling of incompetence.

I knew it well … living it for years. Through the hurt I endured, I developed an imposter persona, replacing a healthy sense of ego with a cloak of shame, which seemed like an impenetrable force field around my ego. Self-love was replaced with a timidity and nonconfrontational attitude that helped protect me. I could be very pleasant and polite. Some of my friends even called me "Eddie Haskell" after the friend of Wally Cleaver in the popular *Leave it to Beaver* TV series of the 1950s and '60s. Eddie was very polite and came off as a young man you would love your son to be around. Behind closed doors, Eddie was mischievous, and a troublemaker—either creating it for others or deep in it himself. He was an imposter.

This Jekyll and Hyde existence characterized who I was. I smashed a fire extinguisher box; led teammates astray through drinking and carousing. I don't remember any Eddie Haskell episode that demonstrated that behavior. Before those two Mr. Hyde moments, the imposter came to a tipping point when I was in eighth grade. I was introduced to students at West Middle School that came from a lot of money. Many of them became friends, and some have been lifelong friends. They lived in a suburb of Denver called Cherry Hills that included a prestigious golf course that has hosted the U.S. Open and other PGA Golf tournaments. I was invited over to one friend's house—a good friend, or so I thought.

We were playing basketball as we loved to do. Two of the other boys started to act like jerks toward me, so much so, I decided to leave. I walked down the street to another house where a group of boys were going to go mess around at Cherry Hills Golf Course. I joined up with them. They were playing a spy type game that turned into so much more.

My anger from being shunned by my friends and the underlying anger of my existence met a perfect storm that night in Cherry Hills, Colorado. We started out sneaking around the course, then we turned to tearing up putting greens by taking flag sticks and ripping them through greens. We took tee markers and threw them through windows of golf maintenance vehicles. I took a large wooden sign and threw it through a maintenance garage window. We were on a roll! We then moved onto the snack shacks, and pried the doors open with sand bunker rakes.

The release of anger I was feeling was exhilarating. We stole beer, cigarettes, sodas, candy bars and whatever else we could get our hands on. We ran to a remote area of the course and stayed for an hour or so, drinking and smoking, coming down from the adrenaline rush of what we had just done. I felt bonded with these boys quickly. I was so desperate to be accepted after what had happened earlier in the night with my other so called friends.

We started to walk back to one of the boy's homes, when the blue and red flashing lights of police cars driving in the golf course area caught our attention. We were able to find our way back to the house unscathed, although the thrill of getting caught had entered my mind. I went to sleep that night with a mind full of guilt and a heart full of shame for what I had done. And I was shaking in my Nikes that I would have to tell my parents. The weight of condemnation and shame wore heavily on me much of that week.

Ultimately, we were outed and charged with trespassing and the destruction of property. I was assigned to 48 hours of community service and ordered to pay restitution for the damage that was done to the golf course. I can still put myself on the floor of that kid's house, with the sinking feeling of despair, disbelief, condemnation, and shame inside of me as I lay there waiting for a new day to come. No matter what you call this shadow self—the imposter, Mr. Hyde—it acts as a protective mechanism that lights you on fire. It is like being inside of a burning house that is collapsing and not realizing that it is burning and collapsing on your head.

How do you stop the self-destruction?

How do you become integrated in your soul and mind?

How do you bring your shadow to the light?

The separation of mind and heart condemns the spirit. An integrated spirit is the place where you can be a starting point for yourself and others. Vulnerability with yourself and others lets your spirit breathe and pours life into it, so you can pour life out. In *Abba's Child*, Brennan Manning puts it this way:

> As we come to grips with our own selfishness and stupidity, we make friends with the imposter and accept that we are impoverished, broken, and realize that if we were not, we would be God. The art of gentleness toward ourselves leads to being gentle with others—and is a natural prerequisite for our presence to God in prayer.

Gentleness toward self is called *forgiveness*. To forgive yourself, it must be in the big things, the little things, and every-thing in between. If you are anything like me, you are hardest on yourself.

**I was at the end of my self-destruction and imposter path.**

Jesus speaking to all people in Matthew 11:28 reveals, "His yoke is easy and His burden is light."

I could not forgive myself on my own, without the experience of Jesus stepping into that yoke with me. On that day in September of 2003, I could not carry anymore burden on my own. My strength had failed. I was at the end of my self-destruction and imposter path. In that moment, I did not feel condemned or critical. I felt rest; I felt at peace. My door was opened to start the healing process from a life full of criticism and condemnation.

My new journey began as I started the walk to become a source of life-giving encouragement, love, and strength. An undeniable substance in the one lives and acts that leads to a purpose-led satisfaction that is rooted deep in one's heart … like an Oak Tree coming to full growth. True freedom had entered my life as I allowed my spirit to lead the way.

The critical spirit and condemnation have no room to manifest when I am focused on being a life generating, and life sustaining, source in this world. When you see yourself as forgiven, for even the worst things you have done—ones that you would not and have not told anyone—your life takes on new meaning. The burden of shame, guilt, condemnation, and the critical spirit lose their power over you. No longer are you alone with your thoughts and emotions.

It takes a certain amount of courage that you may not have summoned before to look deep into how critical you are of yourself and others, and how this creates condemnation. It takes processing your thoughts through writing them down so that you can get proper perspective on what you are thinking. Thoughts trapped in your mind are so much more powerful than when they are on paper.

And it takes the willingness to seek out a trusted confidant who you can go to and tell him or her *everything* ... and that you have been through the Refiners' Fire. Ask that you be steered toward the love of Jesus. This confidant can be a counselor, a person in your recovery group, or a trusted person in your men's or women's group. Birthed from the willingness to change, you will walk away from the critical spirit and condemnation and find a purposeful satisfaction.

> *The greatest legacy one can pass on to one's children and grandchildren is not money or other material things accumulated in one's life but rather a legacy of character and faith.*        —Billy Graham

## coach gus' insights

Think about your legacy often. Are you the type of person, right now, who has the character to help raise future generations to be a source of strength, substance, and life-giving encouragement for others. Have you forgiven yourself so that you can rest and experience freedom through a relationship with Jesus Christ? When you do, the acorn for your growth is in your reach.

# 5 Purposeful Satisfaction

God saw all that he had made, and it was very good. And there was evening, and there was morning—the sixth day.

—Genesis 1:31

# chapter fourteen

# The Shift

*The powerful messaging that we carry*
*can be so harmful and debilitating if left unchecked.*

It was 5:45 a.m. It was early August of 2009. It was another phone call ... another complaint. The project superintendent was grumbling once again because one of my guys had parked in the wrong spot at a job site. As the lead salesperson and manager on a major condominium project, complaints were common considering our scope of work. I was dealing with angry customers, disagreements over pricing, contracts—you name it.

At this point in my life there was a perfect storm of gentle nudges, loud screams, courage, purposeful focusing, and a willingness to risk it all converging on me. Three months earlier, I had committed to the love of my life and started a journey of deeper emotional awareness and building on the character that it takes to be a husband of strength, substance, and life-giving encouragement.

The routine phone calls from the project superintendent before 6 a.m. were the impetus I needed to take the career risk that has come to define the "do over." And I was paying attention. As the gentle nudges from a loving God one year earlier started to be more frequent, a day of golf with John Brooks, one of my best friends, was planned. The destination was Winter Park, 70 miles away. As we headed to the mountains, I shared with him some of the nudges God was giving me.

Now John told me his story of getting his college degree. He was within a few credit hours of completing all the necessary credits but hadn't. Then a trusted friend impressed upon him the importance of finishing. As I listened to John passionately speak about his friend and what was holding him back from taking the final steps, I felt the gravity of the moment for myself. (And yes, he ultimately secured his degree from Colorado State University.) John's friendship has been very significant in my journey to living with purpose and satisfaction. His encouragement and ability to tell me the truth with love has been and continues to be a source of wisdom that I am profoundly grateful for.

I didn't want to have an incomplete to the calls ... the nudges ... that were coming my way. After our round of golf, **At 36, I was definitely in a different place.** I took serious steps in my heart and mind toward following the call that God had for my professional life.

The next day, my repetitive morning complaint calls started at 6 a.m. Another difficult day loomed ahead. Leaning into them, I called Carrie. *Was she available for dinner that evening?*

Knowing that I was frustrated, Carrie listened to my plans with open ears and a warm heart. "Will you give me your blessing in making a career shift?" I asked.

Not only did she but was in full support of the decision, as she has been our entire marriage. My career shift would require me to go back to school to finish my degree and get my teaching license to be in the classroom and coach football. Earlier that summer, Carrie invited me to a networking event where Denver Bronco great Karl Mecklenburg was speaking. His works stuck with me. He said, "If your dream isn't big enough to scare you, then you have to dream bigger!"

My scary dream is to be an NFL head coach someday. With the dream firmly entrenched in my heart and mind, the next step was to conquer the inadequacies and bad memories of my school experience. I graduated from high school with a 1.4 GPA—nothing to brag about. My GPA wasn't indicative of my intellectual capability. It was the result of my ever-present anger and mismanagement of myself during those high school years. And it was all about shame and the story I told myself—the one that I believed.

At 36, I was in a different place. I was responsible. My ability was woven with more experience. Yet with that increased experience, I was headed into waters that I traditionally navigated poorly. To apply to Regis University's online degree and teaching program, I had to write an essay with the application. Write an essay? Are you kidding me? I hadn't written anything longer than purchase orders and short emails to clients for the past twenty years. Writing certainly was not a skill of mine.

I don't remember the topic for the essay, but I do remember how much I struggled organizing, writing with coherent prose, and feeling good about turning in the essay. I spent most of the night writing the essay, and eventually felt confident enough to turn it in along with my application. *Breathe, Britt, I told myself.*

My "do over" was now in motion. Little did I know the catharsis that was to come would be experienced over the next three and a half years. Purposeful satisfaction requires you to take risks that show you who you've always wanted to be, to experience life in ways you didn't think possible. Your life was meant to be lived "full tilt," with maximum energy and inspiration. Did you know that? Few will ever look at starting over to live the way God intended for each of us. Think about it: if you were to check the boxes that include a solid career, a marriage/significant other, maybe children, and a home to call your own, this would be considered "good enough."

I thought the same thing for a long time. Maybe I had further to go than most to achieve "common jerk" status. As I recalled these satisfying life milestones to myself, two men have given me great advice. One of my recovery sponsors gave me wonderful perspective in terms of where we start and where we end. He said, "It doesn't matter if you are a 'common jerk' or what you label yourself, what is important is YOUR path—the one you choose."

My college baseball coach mentioned to me recently, as we spoke about my time with him, that "it doesn't matter how the first and second quarter went. It is how you finish the third and fourth quarter." Ahh ... I had already done the first and second quarters. By starting over, I could live a life of purpose and significance—my third and fourth quarters.

*I let go of comparing myself to others.*

*I let go of "good enough."*

*I grabbed and soaked in forgiveness simultaneously.*

At 47 years old, I am almost to half time if you break down life's quarters into 25 year increments.

I began classes at Regis University in a blended format, split between in person and online learning. In the spirit of "full tilt," I took a full course load—12 credit hours—while working full time in my sales role. In October of 2009, our daughter Isabel was due to be born. At that point I was finishing my first semester of school.

Before Carrie and I were together, she was a corporate executive focused on her work. She had lots of friends and enjoyed traveling the world. I always saw her as a deeply caring and loving woman who had the capacity to be an incredible mother. It was the dominant feature I always observed from her. I don't think many of our friends saw this side of her. Whether she was making food for gatherings, listening intently to one of our friends in conversation, pouring herself out in service to others, or just loving on people, Carrie was Carrie. And I knew that if we ever had children, she would excel at motherhood.

Shortly after we married, we decided that we wanted children ... and soon. The process was not without its difficulties and pain of two miscarriages. Adoption entered our conversation. At this point, I shared a dream I had many years ago with Carrie about holding my child on my shoulders. I was wearing a white t-shirt, with the biggest smile on my face. I could not see the face of my child, but I knew it had been birthed by my wife, whom I did not even know at the time.

I held steadfast to the belief that Carrie and I would have children of our own. I poured this vision into Carrie constantly. In January 2009 we got the solid line on the pregnancy test that confirmed Carrie was pregnant. In the coming days and weeks, we held our breath to see if the egg would implant. When we got to the first doctor's appointment for an ultrasound to see if there was a heartbeat, Carrie was squeezing my hand as hard as she ever had. I was frozen in place in expectancy. As the sonographer ran the wand over Carrie's stomach ... there it was ... a strong and fast heartbeat! Carrie and I burst into tears of joy!

God had given us the gift of Isabel. Purposeful satisfaction had meaning, truth, and a name: Isabel Genevieve Gusmus. We would not see Bel in person for many months, but I knew we would see her. I knew the vision God had given me in that dream would materialize into the child I saw on my shoulders.

On January 17, 2009, I held Carrie's hands and recited our vows. When Carrie looked back at me, a peculiar thing happened. I saw myself so clearly as I looked in her eyes. It was remarkable. We did the same on November 9, 2008, because we wanted to be formally married. We did it front of our church during an intermission of service.

My life was changing dramatically. When you let the God of the Universe be the author of your story, peculiar things will happen. My first semester back in school I took a Western religion class that included visiting a place of worship of one of the big three religions—Judaism, Christianity, Islam—in Western Civilization. I would have a 15-page research paper due in conjunction with the visit. The grade on that paper would be a significant grade in that first semester of work.

I found myself at the Colorado Muslim Community Center to start my project. I spent an afternoon observing and interviewing the men as they went through their daily rituals. The devotion and zeal of their beliefs brought them a purposeful satisfaction. It reminded me of the Refiner's Fire that brought me a devotion and zeal led by love, strength, and substance to the surface of my life. I did not think I would ever find myself in a Muslim community center at any point in my life, let alone writing a research paper about it.

Carrie and I sat in the living room at the end of that first semester waiting for my grades to be posted. The grade to my Western religion paper had been posted. My expectations ranged between mediocrity and just enough to pass. I didn't know anything else as a student, but I got an A! The professor gave me wonderful feedback on my writing prowess.

Being surprised was not what I expected to feel. The joy and elation I felt as I read my grade and feedback to Carrie was transformative. Like high tide coming in and washing away sand to uncover seashells, sand dollars and other treasures buried, going back to school washed away the shame and the belief system of failure that I had held for so long.

The treasure of my intellect and ability to write effectively and my expectations for myself began to rise in a way that was not critical or condemning. Catharsis was in full swing. I could now handle the upheaval of negative emotions because they were being **Purposeful satisfaction came in waves.** rapidly replaced with positive and affirming feedback and action on my behalf. What I missed out on because of the weight and burden I carried was now multiplying affirmation, efficacy, confidence, and freedom. The powerful negative messaging any of us carry can be harmful and debilitating if left unchecked.

Semester after semester, I entered a new experience: a class, a project, and people that solidified for me who I was. I made the Dean's list five times and graduated Magna Cum Laude. Purposeful satisfaction came in waves. There was a total replacement of shame with spirit. With the Holy Spirit leading the way, I became a source of strength, substance, and life-giving encouragement for myself.

This led to a purposeful satisfaction that is difficult to explain, including the hope in this book. This enduring inspiration comes from the reward. If I did not hope beyond hope and believe with all my being that I would have a new experience of life that invigorated me in ways I could never on my own, I would have never chosen this path. The reward is purposeful satisfaction.

In Jesus' parable of the talents in Matthew 25:21, he remarks of the good steward, His master replied,

> *Well done, good and faithful servant!*
> *You have been faithful with a few things;*
> *I will put you in charge of many things.*
> *Come and share your master's happiness!*

Everyone wants to hear the term, *well done*. Where we miss the mark is the next phrase, *good and faithful servant*. Human beings want to be the master, we don't want to be in the subordinate position. There can be no purposeful satisfaction without serving, without stewarding what you have been given with a glad and joyful heart.

As a result of heartache and pain, and self-sabotaging decision making I embraced for years, I did not have many choices left but to do things someone else's way. This may not be your story, though the same principles apply.

Men, if you are not experiencing purposeful satisfaction, if you cannot look in the mirror and say "well done" at this point in your life, look to the source of Kafele for inspiration. The biggest misconception most men experience is this:

**A self-imposed misconception that is blatantly wrong.**

> Men lose something or somehow become inadequate if they are not at the top of the totem pole and seen as an alpha.

This is a self-imposed misconception that is blatantly wrong. With a show of strength and resolve unmatched by any man in the history of the world, Jesus Christ has drawn billions of people to himself with His words … His vision. No man has had the number of followers that starts with a "B" and nine zeroes behind it.

Purpose plus satisfaction is the alignment of experience(s) that change you and your willingness to focus outward instead of inward.

Have you ever had someone look at you with a perplexed look? Not because you have a booger hanging out of your nose or mustard on the side of your lip, but because they have experienced something in your presence or watched you do something out of the ordinary. This does not mean you are special or have superpowers, it means you are living a *peculiar* life.

Carrie and I had a conversation early in our marriage with her Uncle Dennis, the sheriff of Atchison County, Missouri. He mentioned the idea of being peculiar in his marriage with his wife Phyllis. Peculiar to him means "set apart" by God. Dennis and Phyllis surrender and strive to be the example of Kafele, striving to be a source and spreader of seeds that lead strength, substance, and life-giving encouragement. Undeniably, this had led to purposeful satisfaction for both. God sets them apart every day as an example of holiness. Peculiar is such a fitting term, from the perspective of a rare and unusual union that commands respect and honor from those who know them and see them.

It is Carrie's and my belief that God chose us for each other. As a result, we surrender and strive to live a peculiar life together. I often describe our marriage as a fight to get to the banquet table, first elbowing and shoving each other out of the way to get there. Our banquet table, our marriage, symbolizes serving each other. A life lived in service to each other and one another creates purposeful satisfaction.

On October 9, 2009, around 6:30 p.m., Carrie had been given an epidural after heavy contractions. Our Isabel was going to make her debut soon into this world. We sat in the hospital room by ourselves. Carrie was catching her breath between contractions, and I was enjoying the momentary calm and reflecting on our journey to get to this point.

After our first miscarriage, I was trying to come to grips with the loss of our child and how I cared for Carrie during this time. My response was one of complete insensitivity and meat-headedness in which I had excelled. At the time, I did not have the character it took to be an oak tree. The oak tree concept wasn't in my mental bandwidth.

At the end of Carrie's pregnancy, I was asked to go play in a softball tournament that landed on the day after Isabel was born. My first thought was, *I need to go play in this tournament.* My mom, who has always been a supportive and wise force in my life, said, "That is a bad decision."

After waffling for a few minutes, I called the manager of the team I was going to play for and said, "There is another lineup I want to be in, the most important lineup of my life." I did not go to that game. I firmly planted myself with Carrie and Isabel. I had a lot to learn regarding being an Oak Tree Source.

> Meatheadedness ... not a word in the dictionary, but it is a perfect adjective for my lack of compassion that day. From that day to sitting on the precipice of having a child, I was not the same person. I was humbled, honored, and expected to be a wonderful father and compassionate husband. I committed to stand strong like an oak tree.

Carrie and I chose not to learn the sex of our baby before birth. We had names selected for a son or a daughter. The time was imminent, and I stood by Carrie' side and held her hand as she courageously delivered our beautiful baby to the world. The doctor received the baby and stood, handing the crying infant to me. I will never forget that moment. She was a sweet baby girl, Isabel ... Isabel Genevieve Gusmus.

*Show me a thoroughly satisfied man and I will show you a failure.*

—Thomas Edison

# coach gus' insights

If you settle for a life that is *good enough,* there will always be a hunger for more. If you are not afraid to do the work that it takes to experience purposeful satisfaction, the hunger of your masculine heart will be fulfilled.

# chapter fifteen

# Creating Purposeful Satisfaction

*Significance hit me
right between the eyes my first year of teaching.*

It was no longer about me, or Carrie and me … it was about so much more. In that moment purpose and satisfaction met in a glorious quickening. Just like the thrill of hearing Izzy's heartbeat the first time, meeting her in person deepened the roots of God's oak tree growing in me.

Carrie gave me a couple of looks and a gesture during this time that have given me a depth and breadth of experience in this life that can only be categorized as divine. The first one was when I had just given Bel to the nurse to get her cleaned up and placed in the warming incubator and turned to Carrie. We locked eyes with a beautifully meaningful gaze of satisfaction that flowed between the two of us—our lives were worth living.

The second occurred one night during that winter of 2009, after we had arrived home with Isabel. I was firmly entrenched in school, becoming the source of strength and substance my "girls" needed. I was holding Bel and Carrie gazed into my eyes with tears in hers and gave me an enormous hug. Nothing needed to be said. I knew exactly what Carrie meant. This was an important moment in our young love.

A few days after those moments, I just stopped in my tracks with an overwhelming sense of satisfaction with everything happening in my life. The rush of joy and depth of what human existence was meant to be overcame me. It was as if everything I had gone through to that point in my life had converged in that moment to give me a gift of purposeful satisfaction. That moment in the winter of 2009 with these affirmations hitting my heart with such significance is a big part of the reason this book is being written.

**You may never be in a position for a *do over*.**

Too many times I tried to control or force goodness and gladness into my life. Whether it was a relationship, an accomplishment, or generally not trying to hate myself, the harder I tried to experience purposeful satisfaction … the harder everything became. *Soulful Parenting* author Susan Gale captures my struggles well. "Sometimes we need to just make peace with our past in order for our future not to become a constant battle."

It was time for me to hit the reset button so that I didn't have to fight myself any longer, so that I could live *full tilt*. Early in sobriety, I thought I had to play "catch up" because I still believed I was missing or lacking something. The truth is you may never be in a position for a *do over*. A reset does become pivotal to make peace with your past if you are the common denominator in leaving wreckage with people, places, and things. That transition surfaces with your awareness and acknowledgment that *you* hold the wrecking ball.

> You may have come to a place in your life where you crave more—more substance, more strength, and more purpose in how you live. My hope as you read my story is that you become inspired to live with purpose and significance that will result in purposeful satisfaction.

An essential component to attain purposeful satisfaction is a willingness, a courage, to be broken, to unlearn or let go of beliefs that keep you anchored to a "good enough" living. You need to unlearn destructive behaviors that hurt you and those around you. Brokenness is about removing anything that stands in the way of you loving yourself, seeing yourself, and your unique worth, and the way you were created by the God of the Universe, just as Brennan Manning so masterfully and inspirationally captured in *Abba's Child*.

I don't know where I would be without that revelation in my life. I was a receptionist slash customer service manager at the Keller Williams Real Estate Company from 1998 to 2003. Our managing broker wanted to institute the Ritz Carlton service greeting: "It's a great day at the Ritz Carlton. How may I assist you?" This phrase is part of my legacy. We put it in place at our branch in the Denver Tech Center.

I became known around the city by real estate agents for the greeting. Agents and clients would come in to meet me. Many, many times people remarked about their first experience with Keller Williams DTC being so important to them. The greeting, my presence, my service orientation, the care and concern I showed for people became a staple of the KW DTC experience. As I wrote this line in 2021, I decided to call the branch. Sure enough, it still uses the greeting.

From what may have seemed to be a corny idea and not that original, with enthusiasm and passion, I created purposeful satisfaction for others that lives on 20 years later. It's time to ask: What is that idea you have that will create purpose and satisfaction for you … for others? It's time to go after it!

When I walked across that stage to receive my diploma combined with a teaching certificate in May of 2012, the chapter that started as a boy had been a Groundhog Day too long. It ended and the new man walking across that stage was me. An era of inadequacy, frustration, and a shameful narrative that had seeped into every area of my life was over. What surfaced was a man infused with victory, affirmation, efficacy, strength, substance and ultimately deliverance into purposeful satisfaction.

I felt invincible. I was on such a roll after finishing my undergraduate degree, and looking for a full-time teaching job, that I enrolled in the Master of Education program at Regis University. The degree focus was curriculum, assessment, and instruction. I finished the two-year program in one year and started my first full-time teaching job. It is amazing what operating from enthusiasm, passion, and confidence led by purpose can do. Purposeful satisfaction flowed through me.

Significance hit me right between the eyes in my first year of teaching. Many days felt like I had been in a meat grinder— my mind was ground up, my emotions were ground down— but there was a pull toward the work that was significant. If you didn't mind connecting with kids in a meaningful way at 10:30 a.m. then getting cussed out by them at lunchtime, the work was significant. Stepping into the lives of young men and women who faced challenges that no one should ever have to pulls you toward that innate human response to help.

Even in the chaos, and emotional and mental stress, the job at Compassion Road Academy (CRA), an alternative Denver Public School high school, helped me focus on moments of small breakthroughs. Purposeful satisfaction cannot be felt without the moments of breakthrough that capture your frailty and reveals your strength. In my experience, rarely has it been the quick type of transformational moments that reveal purposeful satisfaction, rather the time spent in trial and error and challenge where purposeful satisfaction becomes obvious.

When I look back at my time at CRA, I was not prepared for what was to come. What was revealed was satisfaction of purpose that reached far beyond the classroom—and my expectations. As a source (starting point) and spreader of the seeds of strength, substance, and life-giving encouragement, I often think about the impact of how I live, and the message I send.

> A purposefully satisfied life screams for the creation of belonging and connection.

Today, I am friends with many of my former students on social media. They graduated and are thriving as young adults. With former students following my social media pages, it is important that I have an eye on eternity for young people, and not only young people, but every person I come in contact with. I hope they feel and witness the enthusiasm, passion, substance and strength I operate with and by. Everybody deserves your loving, encouraging, graceful self every day, especially the person staring back at you in the mirror.

The byproduct of a purposefully satisfied life screams for the creation of belonging and connection. If this type of satisfaction sounds interesting, ask THE source of life to walk into your room and make things new. When you have been made new, you don't need to be blessed because YOU are the blessing. In the Kingdom of God, and its counterintuitive nature, being the blessing allows you to receive blessing. Self-sacrifice, not self-promotion, clears the way for you to experience freedom mentally, emotionally, and spiritually. I was given a hat by my mother-in-law that had the Superman emblem and Super Jesus stitched in the middle. Jesus is the superhero of my life. By His sacrifice, He is the blessing to me … to so many. With the same attitude in mind, I sacrificed my superficial wants and desires to have His wants and desires for me that have created purposeful satisfaction.

*A life isn't significant except for its impact on other lives.*
                                                              —Jackie Robinson

## coach gus' insights

It is the moments that stop you in your tracks that need your attention, which need you to lean into so that you can have a more meaningful experience.

# chapter sixteen

# Going Back to Go Forward

*Gaining insight, knowledge, and perspective
allows your purpose to emerge, become clearer,
or be positively reinforced.*

I am a person who thrives from context and believes history and one's personal history can help fill in gaps in your own existence. It can launch you forward with another layer of solid foundation in your identity. It's what Carrie, our kids, and I did on a recent road trip to the southern United States. Who was I? Where did I come from? What inspired my ancestors? It was time to find out about the Gusmus family lineage.

As I stood next to the graves of my great grandfather Frank J. Gusmus, my great-great grandfather Louis Gusmus, and my great-great-great grandfather and Gusmus family Patriarch John Conradus Gusmus, I could not help but feel connected. Even though those men had passed on, I knew I was standing on hallowed ground that was significant to me and my story. It was part of my fabric … of the Gusmus clan that migrated to Colorado.

The rest of the day we spent with my cousin Pat Staley. Pat is the keeper of the Gusmus historical record. The day was filled with stories, pictures, and moments that filled my cup and gave context to where I came from. To hear about the attitudes, the behaviors, and the lives these men and women led was fascinating. John Conradus Gusmus came to America by way of Galveston Bay, Texas, with other families who were able to purchase land. He arrived in Texas in 1845, the year Texas became a state. My great-great-great grandfather married and became a landowner shortly after he settled.

As a direct descendent, I am eligible to become part of the first family of Texas. I don't know about you but having a shot at being royalty is one you've got to take. Even though it is just a certificate you receive, royalty is royalty. To know where we are going, we need to know where we came from. With a narrow view of the men in my family and a view that I did not always **Their history is** connect with, taking the dive into the **part of your being.** Gusmus ancestors gave me perspective that is invaluable for my life today and going forward.

Gaining insight, knowledge, and perspective allows your purpose to emerge, become clearer, or be positively reinforced. By learning detailed accounts regarding the Gusmus men and women, their discipline, their entrepreneurial spirit, and their giving hearts reinforced the purpose that I live with.

During the Great Depression, Louis and Frank Gusmus owned a general store, a Walmart of sorts during the 1930s. They gave credit to people in the Muscle Shoals, Alabama area for groceries and supplies when they could not afford them. When Louis died in 1934, the Gusmus General Store died with him. People thought that they did not need to pay their debts after his death. To know that the Gusmus men gave in the hardest of times reinforces my belief that my family and I have enough. And we live from the overflow of the blessings of God.

That doesn't mean material blessings, even though Carrie and I have lived from material blessing. More importantly, it's the blessing of God's presence, guidance, and love in our lives. It seems my Gusmus family knew that they'd be taken care of when they gave sacrificially. I cannot recommend with more conviction to seek out the men in your surname's history. If you need to make peace with them, do it. If you have only been told parts of the story or have the urge in you to connect with something bigger than yourself, there is no better place to start than your family of origin. Their history is part of your being.

**There is a purity in encouragement that stands in stark contrast to sarcasm.**

It brings me immense joy and purposeful satisfaction that my children have never seen me drink alcohol or smoke cigarettes, and by the grace of God, I pray that they never will. As a disciple of Jesus, I expect myself to be the model of what "TO DO" instead of the devious Eddy Haskell type. Do you live for the one-liners, the sarcastic remark that will get a great laugh and put your cleverness on display? I did.

Does anger and anxiety lurk right under the surface of your emotions or thoughts? When others, including those closest to you, touch a nerve, do you back them up or take their knees out with your words? I did. We have all been there, when our words become weapons, we become dividers and not uniters. Your words either give life or take it away.

There is a purity in encouragement that stands in stark contrast to sarcasm. Don't get me wrong, I like to joke and poke fun in a Dad joke sort of way. But you can't communicate both ways. You can't divide in one breath and unite in another. This is double speak, deliberately distorting words and/or playing on words to disguise their meaning. Direct confrontation becomes nonexistent. When sarcasm is used, authenticity is kept at a distance. Those sharp, bitter, and deriding comments are designed to mock and ridicule. It is widely accepted in American male culture that these types of comments are signs of love to our friends, just like a backhanded compliment.

The truth: It may show off your wit and your intellect, but it cuts your friend. And it's harmful. Your friends may never admit that your remarks were hurtful. Their thick skin shields them from appearing soft. Wrong. What is soft is using passive aggressive jabs where you want to make a point, or be honest with someone, yet you don't have the courage to communicate directly with that person. This accepted and embraced culture of sarcasm is killing men slowly. It is keeping us from our authentic power.

I am reminded of the Heisman Trophy pose when I hear sarcasm. We have one hand out, stiff arming others with sarcasm, while protecting the ball—our hearts from letting authenticity in—and running away. These interactions used to bother me with friends, maybe because my wit is not sharp. But I expected more depth and authenticity from my friends.

The reciting of underdog stories makes me think of sarcasm as a type of double speak. The underdog can be anyone … maybe you. It's the person who must overcome the odds, the ridicule, the doubters, to win. There is such purposeful satisfaction in overcoming the odds. Movies like *Rocky, The Karate Kid, Hoosiers,* and *Rudy* all helped shape my understanding of purposeful satisfaction as it connects to the Hero's Journey.

When you allow yourself to become part of the bigger story —the one that Jesus Christ died for—the way you speak, the way your nonverbal communication presents you, transforms you and those around you. The truth: You will have no need to keep others at arm's length because vulnerability and candor will be something you and others yearn for. Connection to your brothers takes on a new meaning. When you look people in the eye, you don't need to be defensive or exert your will over them. When you look into the eyes of others, you should exude confidence and an inviting spirit. The quicker your desire to connect and bring people into your circle, the quicker you will experience purposeful satisfaction.

A major stumbling block to purposeful satisfaction can be "offense." When you let people rent space in your mind, it becomes a corrosive thread that prevents you from experiencing the satisfaction of living your purpose. John Bevere writes in his book *The Bait of Satan,* "Offense cuts you off from God. We separate ourselves from the pipeline. I've never seen anything block blessings except offense."

Having gone through the Refiner's Fire to burn out the impurities in my own life, a burning that revealed that God could build His kingdom within me, the double speak of Satan tested that obedience to God. While interviewing for the head football coaching job at my current school, it seemed that the decision on who would get the position was made before the interviews had even started. I was offended. This meant that the interviews meant nothing and were unnecessary. Others outside of the interview committee had the necessary influence as to who would get the final position. It wasn't me.

After the process was over and I had calmed down, the new head coach asked me to be the assistant head coach. I accepted. What transpired during that season was a true exercise in submittal and obedience so that I would not become offended.

**I was going to support this senior class.** The head coach and I did not see eye-to-eye on many things. Most of all, how to treat players. I had been with this group of seniors since their sophomore year. They naturally looked to me as the familiar coach among an unfamiliar staff. During summer workouts, I never thought I would have to make a choice between allegiance to the players, namely the seniors, or to the new head football coach.

This is exactly what it came down to. The honeymoon phase with him was fading quickly. I sensed that the seniors were feeling the motives of this new coach were less than encouraging and that they questioned them. There was a moment for me that defined that season and shifted my focus even though it was difficult not to be offended. The senior quarterback asked me to come out with him and some of the wide receivers for a throwing session. I did not tell our head coach that I was going to do this. They trusted me; they needed my support. And I committed to meet them on the field, and we had a great session.

Yes, I knew he would not be happy that work was getting done without clearing it with him first. And, that he could be offended that I did not tell him. That decision, though, became the core of most every decision I made throughout that season ... my lens. *I was going to support this senior class.* My motto as a coach and teacher has always been and will always be, "It is about the kids." At the cost of being treated as the outcast or possibly being fired, I would be a source of strength, substance, and life-giving encouragement to that senior class.

The season continued to be a struggle. I fought off being offended by what seemed to be thrown at me daily. While supporting the kids, I encouraged them to be good teammates to the younger players and build their character because of this difficult situation I was experiencing. I relied on the insights from John Bevere's *The Bait of Satan.* Throughout, it references scripture, specifically 1 Peter 4:12,

*I am determined to daily exercise my spirit that I may strengthen my heart, mind and emotions, so that I will not be so vulnerable to the hurt of others.*

The subtitle of the Bevere book said it all: Living free from the deadly trap of offense.

At every turn, people, places, and things are the mirror for you to examine yourself. Not only was I a source of strength, substance, and life-giving encouragement for the senior class, I was those things for myself, my family, and those around me. As a result of focusing on being a source of strength, substance, and life-giving encouragement, I did not become cut off from the pipeline of blessing. I felt it.

During the 2019 season, I landed at a new high school as its quarterback coach. Rod Sherman was the head coach and became a mentor and a friend. He was a five time state champion coach whose character, vision, leadership, and ability to run a team were exactly what I needed. Earlier this year, the coach that had been at the previous school I coached at ended up leaving because of some of the same issues that plagued his first year: his treatment of kids and creation of a hostile environment.

Intrigued with the news and confident in myself, I applied for the position again at the school. After all, I'd been there for four years as an in-building coach; had a sterling reputation for hard work and loyalty; and had a tremendous standing among the players and student body. In addition, the interview committee was made up of many of my colleagues and people I believed were advocates. They weren't and I did not get the job. The disappointment, hurt, and potential to be offended and unforgiving was palpable. So much so, that I dreamed of the time when I would be an opposing head coach and playing this school and winning, scoring 100 points in that game! (It is incredibly difficult to score 100 points in a football game.)

Carrie was upset. We argued because of the emotionally charged investment I had made when I applied and our paths for each other and successes we've achieved. The school I was at has a storied football tradition, and a prideful attitude when it comes to football. Plus, there is no shortage of politics when it comes to a proud football school. None. Not being a head coach before played into the decision. My paper resume was not as expansive as some of the other candidates.

What I did have was the commitment and leadership across all levels of the school from the administration to the maintenance crew that I provided. My reputation with the kids was rich, respectful, and very meaningful. Not only did I have the kids respect in the classroom but on the field of play as well. Even though the school had seen me in action for an extended period of time and had multiple testimonies of my good works from many people, the committee did not see what I've actually done in person. Their choice was to honor a piece of paper.

It is difficult to accept that you are evaluated on what a resume says and not the work you have done. By this point in my experience at this school, I was not offended, but I was disappointed that my dream and call at this school had not come to be. Proverbs tells this story of my call and tells the story of purposeful satisfaction:

> *Hope deferred makes the heart sick,*
> *but a longing fulfilled is a tree of life.*
> —Proverbs 13:12

Yes, my heart was sick, and as of the time of this writing still is on some level. But God has given me the "tree of life." He has given me the message of the Oak Tree Source to practice and share through this work. My satisfaction does not lie in my title, my position, my influence or following. Yet, my imposter will tell me it does, and sometimes I listen. And then the Holy Spirit leads me to the truth that I have come to rely on.

I don't know what my coaching future holds, or if anyone will connect with the message of the Oak Tree Source as I have. What I do know, without a doubt, is that purposeful satisfaction lies in living focused on consequential contributions to this world as a result of becoming a source of strength, substance, and life-giving encouragement to others.

While I have experienced heartbreak, as you have, the opportunities to contribute significantly have been many. The private school offers a spiritual retreat that lets boys and girls engage in reflection of Catholic/Christian spirituals, while doing some deep dives into their own story. I have had the privilege and blessing the last four years to kick off the boys' retreat in December by telling my story ... the peaks and valleys, and the in between.

> **You can never underestimate the power of going back to go forward.**

For the students to observe a grown man become radically vulnerable and seriously honest about his life and have the story of redemption and victory to go along with it, gave my relationship with hundreds of boys an anchor that can never be taken away.

*We cry together.*

*We pray together.*

*We worship together.*

The significance and purposeful satisfaction that I craved for my career was being realized. The sum of my experiences was being used to help young boys become men and to discover, uncover, and discard things about themselves that will serve them for decades and hopefully eternity. The purposeful satisfaction I encountered through sharing my experiences with them gave me a new lens to view myself.

> It's like God planned it that way. As I spoke about the shame, guilt, and pain, I was no longer that boy. Instead, I was a man who could take care of that boy now. You can never underestimate the power of going back to go forward.

Years ago, I was a first year offensive coordinator. It was our rival game for the neighborhood trophy. We had lost the previous year, badly. We were 1-2 heading into the game. I have always believed that running the screen game at the high school level would always be a positive yardage play and in many instances a game breaking play. In our first three games we had run I-Right HB Slip R—a screen pass to the running back with a wall of blockers in front of him—a handful of times and had positive yardage each time. But we had not broken a big gain that I had expected. In the second quarter of that game, I called the HB Slip, and our tail back broke it for a sixty yard touchdown. As he broke into the open field, I sprinted with him down the sideline the last forty yards. The way I expected the play to work always created joy and purposeful satisfaction in me that I could not contain. The referee warned me about stepping out of the coach's box.

At that moment, I could not have cared less.

How much unresolved hurt and hang ups do you have … emotionally, mentally, spiritually? You will stuff that stuff with all the will power you can muster. But, when you taste the freedom that comes along with resolution and ministering to yourself in ways you did not think possible, you start to become solid and powerful oak trees.

It is not enough to move away from pain. The goal is to move toward purpose, so life becomes purposefully satisfying. If you believe that experiencing catharsis and resolution are a passive and not an active experience of dynamic forces at work, then you have most likely looked in the mirror and said, "Everything is fine."

Living life with an authoritative presence doesn't mean you exert your will over people, places, and things. It means that you have a confidence about you that commands respect. There is no need to shout and overbear, demean, or domineer. In a world starved for connection and authenticity, you can no longer show up as a shell of yourself or a projection of what others think you should be. Taking offense, over sensitivity, self-centeredness, approval seeking, passive aggressiveness, and leading with your imposter, enable you to keep the "everything is fine" allusion alive and well.

I have come to a place where I expect the best will happen for me. If my hope remains alive, my dreams and longings will be fulfilled, and I will experience the tree of life. Purposeful satisfaction creates joy from the journey and the chase, and the surrender, the trial by the Refiner's Fire.

Even when you are disappointed, feeling doubtful, and your ability to be expectant of the best coming, never stop chasing purposeful satisfaction once you've tasted it. Settling for "good enough" and "everything is fine" no longer becomes an option.

*Most of the important things in the world have been accomplished by people who have kept trying when their seemed to be no hope at all.*  —Dale Carnegie

## coach gus' insights

No matter how difficult the active pursuit of purposeful satisfaction becomes, keep putting one foot in front of the other and run your race. Breakthrough is one step away.

# 6 Rearrangement

Do not conform to the pattern of this world but be transformed by the renewing of your mind. Then you will be able to test and approve what God's will is—his good, pleasing and perfect will.

—Roman 12:2

# chapter seventeen

# Rearrangement ... Creating a Life of Being

*As strange as it may seem,*
*what has always worked doesn't always work.*

When Christmas time and the holidays arrive, most families have one of two kinds of experiences. Either it is wonderful, warm, and loving, or utter chaos and dismay with members of the family having issues of some sort. They might ask, "Can we never let Uncle Steve drink too much again because he made an ass out of himself and stirred up everybody else in the process?"

The holidays for me were mostly a pleasant time spent with my family. The gatherings got smaller and smaller as the years went on. I always loved to see my grandparents, and when they passed away, the urgency to hold big gatherings diminished. Dad's birthday is on Christmas Eve, and that always gave us more reason to celebrate. For years, he would have friends over and celebrate it; gatherings I always enjoyed.

For many families, the holidays are painful memories of arguments and fractures in family relationships that are sometimes irreparable. These memories leave scars, and hang ups that are only magnified when Thanksgiving, Christmas, and New

**Oh, I knew the power of hallucinations ...**

Year's come around that should bring love and hope, but they bring stress and pain. This stress and pain can sit for years inside of you if you don't take action to have a new experience ... a celebration and a forthcoming new year.

I got clean and sober in 2005. Over Christmas/New Year's from 2005 to 2007, I experienced something that I can only explain as a "rearrangement." When you think of rearranging something, maybe it's your living room furniture, or your sock drawer, or the guy riding your bumper in traffic when there is no place to go.

The rearrangement I experienced during this time, and still do to a certain degree today, was that of Jesus Christ laying the foundation of his kingdom in me. I remember the feeling vividly of being lost and mesmerized at the same time. Now read the previous statement again and you might say, "This guy just came off of using drugs and was hallucinating from having substance out of his system." But, oh, I knew the power of hallucinations ... and these new experiences became far more of an anchor for me mentally, emotionally, spiritually than psychological chemical substances.

And yes, at the time this was happening, I did not feel anchored at all. But this "thing" had my attention. I was no longer doing things the way I used to do them. I was different in how I felt inside and what my behaviors became on the outside. This made possible a way for everything to change, for everything to be rearranged. From the perspective of the experience I was having with myself, what was happening was so odd.

Obviously, I was in control of the function of my physical body and my thoughts, yet there was the subtle undercurrent of something happening that I had no control over.

When it came to the word *rearrangement*, Jung described it as:

> Ideas, emotions, and attitudes which were once the guiding forces of the lives of these men are suddenly cast to one side, and a completely new set of conceptions and motives begin to dominate them.

These conversations and treatment sessions led to the birthing of Alcoholics Anonymous and the essential principle that helps A.A. be successful. Jung mentions that alcoholics have recovered by a *vital spiritual experience*. He means having a rearrangement and/or emotional displacement. Even though this rearrangement did not happen for me all in one quickening of my

**My identity was no longer held hostage by failure and shame of something I loved—my do over of life.**

soul, the undeniable change in emotions, attitude, and ideas set me on my personal *do over* of life. After a lifetime of rearranging and adjusting my life to try and "fit in," "be approved of," "make meaning," "control" people, places, and things, I created *one way of being*.

I remember having conversations with my psychologist about my desire not to be "just an athlete and my life related to sports by everyone." I was so much more than who I was as an athlete. Plus, sports, for me, I believed were a failure. It was no wonder I did not want my identity seen through that lens. As the displacement of shame, guilt, inadequacy, self-hatred were cast aside, I began to focus in a more precise way. My identity was no longer held hostage by failure and shame of something I loved—my do over of life. It was okay to have more of a narrow focus and purpose. By no means do I consider myself narrow in my emotions, ideas, and attitudes. Instead of "falling for everything" that I referred to in earlier chapters, I was replaced with insight that gave me the freedom to make decisions based on a new set of principles.

> When you hold onto what you know so tight, you miss the opportunities to grow new roots and build new branches that would help you, such as the idea that men have a set of rules, responsibilities, and norms they must live by, and women have a completely opposite set of rules they embrace. When it comes to physiological makeup and emotional makeup, I understand there are real differences.

If you are willing to have a new experience of yourself, and others, and the way others perceive you, there will be room for innovative ideas, attitudes, and emotions. As strange as it may seem, what has always worked doesn't always work. You get in enough pain and don't want to experience it anymore. Your circumstances have changed, or your lack of flexibility has alienated you from others. There comes a day of reckoning when your skillset doesn't fit your job description any longer. The people in your life have grown and matured and you don't connect with them the way you used to.

At that point, you have a choice to make. You can begin the process of letting go and letting rearrangement take place in your life, or you can continue to get the results you have always gotten.

The benefits of becoming flexible in how you operate cannot be understated. To be a source of strength, substance, and life-giving encouragement, you need to understand that there is not a one-size-fits-all method. When Jesus Christ performed miracles, gathered and trained his apostles, he was constantly in the moment, flexible enough to see that interactions with others called for flexible responses.

> *And he began to teach them that the Son of Man*
> *must suffer many things and be rejected by the elders*
> *and the chief priests and the scribes and be killed,*
> *and after three days rise again.*
> —Mark 8:31-32

And he said this plainly. Then, Peter took Jesus aside and began to rebuke him. But turning and seeing his disciples, he rebuked Peter and said,

> *Get behind me, Satan!*
> *For you are not setting your mind on the things of God,*
> *but on the things of man." With this pointed rebuke*
> *of Satan, we see that Jesus had his heart and spirit wide*
> *open and ready to act with authority and truth.*
> —Mark 8:33

In another instance, we see Him speaking to the Samaritan woman at the well. Jesus answers her,

*If you knew the gift of God, and who it is that is saying to*
*you, 'Give me a drink,' you would have asked him, and he*
*would have given you living water." The woman said to*
*him, "Sir, you have nothing to draw with, and the well is*
*deep; where do you get that living water? Are you greater*
*than our father Jacob, who gave us the well and drank from*
*it himself, and his sons and his cattle?" Jesus said to her,*
*"Everyone who drinks of this water will thirst again, but*
*whoever drinks of the water that I shall give him will never*
*thirst; the water I shall give him will become in him*
*a spring of water welling up to eternal life.*
—John 4: 11-14

Not only does Jesus illustrate a core truth of who he is with
an invitation, but offers "living water" and a spring welling up
inside of us of eternal life. With love, compassion, and authority
that only He could exude, Jesus Christ shows flexibility and the
ability to rearrange our ideas, attitudes, and emotions. Led by
the Holy Spirit, Jesus was ready for any situation, and had the
righteous action, thought, word that pierced the heart of everyone he encountered.

Wouldn't you like your influence, your inspiration to touch
the heart? From the heart comes the spring of eternal life, Jesus.
If you want to touch hearts and inspire minds, you cannot be
the same person you have been. The hardest thing for you and
others to do, is do something someone else's way. How many
times has that little ping of pride inside hit you when someone
says, "You might want to try it this way" or your wife says, "This
is not the way I wanted this done." How you manage these situations says a lot about your ideas, attitudes, and emotions.

I find it essential to separate myself from my perspective, which helps give me a true perspective. It is like standing beside yourself, bringing to light a reflective conscience that "notices" those things about yourself that you don't notice day in and day out. I liken it to watching film with my players, as they get to see themselves apart from practice, and their own perspective. I get to stand beside them to be that reflective conscience for them as they improve.

As you look deeper and wider at your experience, along with others' experience of you, you can see where you can minister to yourself and really make transformational change that helps you, and others, become a source of strength, substance, and life-giving encouragement. **If I knew then what I know now ...** When I was a boy, trying to become a man, I needed so desperately to be able to minister to myself in a compassionate, loving, and accountable way. I didn't do a good job of it, lacking the tools and skills to take me to that level of transformation.

As I write this, I am reminded of the powerful lyrics Mercy Me created in "Dear Younger Me" that opens with the line: *If I knew then what I know now ...,*

> When you know what you need to carry and what you don't need to carry, ministering to yourself takes on a whole new meaning. Hindsight is always 20/20, yet the ministry and healing you can do within is miraculous if you are willing. Even if you believe your actions are not hurting anyone but yourself, your actions have lasting effects on others. Andy Andrews, author of *The Noticer: Sometimes, All a Person Needs Is a Little Perspective*, puts it this way,

> While it is true that most people never see or understand the difference they make, or sometimes only imagine their actions having a tiny effect, every single action a person takes has far-reaching consequences.
>
> A spiritual rearrangement that moves you from a set of ideas, attitudes, and emotions that involve condemnation and shame to awareness, compassion, love, and a larger perspective are vital to seeing the impact and difference you make each day. When you see your impact because of a reflective conscious and ditch ideas that no longer serve you, your impact can multiply and start to bring people along.

If you, and other men, dream of leading, influencing, motivating, this is why there are thousands of books on leadership and autobiographies of top level leaders who have won wars, won championships, and won capitalism. None of it matters if you have not brought people with you, creating a legacy that will live past your time on earth. Few of us will have books written about us, but you can write a book about the story of your journey. Every journey is unique. This is for a reason. You have a story that only you can tell.

*Your story* is worth being told. To tell it, there must be a compelling *why*. Why you made the decisions you made. Why you took a risk here and not there. You will inevitably bump into ceilings in your life. What you are willing to accept is the measure of satisfaction and meaning you will experience. Those ceilings represent the opportunities for rearrangement, to replace those beliefs that have become weights with new ones that become your new anchors.

During one Kairos retreat, I was doing the work so that I could break through another ceiling when the God of the Universe decided to drop in and give me an affirmation of His presence in my life. The first morning of the retreat, I walked toward the meeting hall with a reflective conscious and a heavy heart. Under attack from the enemy of my soul, I received a glimpse, just like the glimpse of purposeful satisfaction, as I walked through our home. This glimpse was another inspiration of the worth of discovering, uncovering, and discarding the ideas, attitudes, and emotions that keep you from the best you can be. The distinct difference between your mind and thoughts and the spirit of God living within you is the difference between life lived in expectancy and life lived in uncertainty.

On the last day of the retreat, the participants had some down time in the afternoon. In all the years I have attended, the last day is special to me. It's when I go to the beautiful Spanish style chapel on the property and sit for a while and speak to God, just the two of us. Every time, I am moved to tears. I have such a passion for God, for life, for people. This happened because of the vital spiritual experiences I've had over time.

On this day, I walked down to the chapel, sat, and spoke with God. After all the thoughts and emotions that had gone through me this past week, I knew I needed to do more writing. When the upheaval comes, writing is a fantastic way to take the power from your mind to paper that diffuses the power your thoughts and emotions have over you so that the truth can be revealed. Music is in the background when I write, and there was a certain song I wanted to listen to, but I could not remember the song. Usually, when I am in the space to write, the songs

I want to listen to come to mind quickly. I didn't think much of the song escaping my mind until we were in Friday afternoon mass, and the song came on as we finished taking communion.

I was stopped in my tracks as the Chris Rice song, "Untitled Hymn," started playing. I firmly believe that God winks at us sometimes to give us an "atta boy" or "atta girl" so that we know our prayers, our seeking, our sacrifice, our hearts are loved more than we could possibly know. As I stood and soaked in God's glory, the weight of my mind and emotions were replaced by praise and the shine of the presence of Him. Knowing that I needed to share this little piece of experienced glory, the 50 plus boys and 10 or so adults in the chapel that evening all received a "glory" hug from me.

As each exited, I squeezed him and said, "This is a little glimpse of God's glory." It is customary in the Catholic faith to exchange handshakes and embraces and say, "Peace be with you." That night, it was "Glory be with you." The experiences I've had with God have been glorious. There is no doubt about it.

There isn't a year when my faith hasn't been tested. Sometimes, I wonder if these experiences are overemotional expressions, or my mind is desiring a certain outcome. Have you ever had doubts as to whether God is involved personally in your life? I have. When that doubt surfaced, I would ask myself:

*Was I in such desperate need of rearrangement that I would believe anything?*

*Was the still small voice just the voice of my conscience*
*nudging me forward to follow my dreams and purpose?*

When you doubt yourself and your experiences, you take
away the opportunity for sober perspective. When you question
the experiences that have helped shape your perspective, there is
no room for spirituality, let alone God to minister to you.

You can minister to yourself because God ministered to all
of us first. A life lived with and for God is an all-in proposition.
You don't get to pick and choose what you agree and disagree
with. When you are discouraged and climb back on the throne
of your old life and proclaim that God is "not real" and "not
loving" or "why would God let this happen" or "not let that happen," you shortchange yourself and limit your opportunities.

When doubt increases and climbs to almost a fever pitch, or
when the enemy for your soul is pulling out all the stops to keep
you bound, where do you turn? Start with the truth, the word of
God in His inspired text, without fail. It ministers to me every
time I open it. Each year, Carrie and I read the entire Bible and
then share what we each take away at the end of the day. The
Bible comes alive for me most mornings with a new connection,
a fresh word spoken. When any doubt creeps into my thoughts
and feelings, my soul is crying out for something this world
cannot give me.

Once you have gotten a glimpse of holiness, you will never
be the same. The tricks and schemes of the enemy have no credibility when they are held next to the glory of God. As I wrote
that line, there was a new level of truth that hit my heart. Not
only does discouragement and doubt not hold up to glory, but

*glory* holds you and me up and sets apart the platform so that God, Jesus, and the Holy Spirit are exalted.

With rearrangement and displacement of my ideas, attitudes, thoughts and emotions, I have found that I expect the best outcome, the best situations to come about in my life. I believe you will, too. Living in expectancy allows you to overcome dis-

**Rearrangement does not happen without an upheaval.**

couragement and disappointment with regularity and no loss of enthusiasm. Having seen the other side, exhilaration, excitement, and enthusiasm have become who I am. You may be thinking, *This guy lives in his little utopia and doesn't consider reality.*

There is no denying the reality of life as it is in the moment. I am not immune to the decisions of people, places, and things. In fact, what I cannot control is a great exercise in the discipline it takes to live from expectancy. Your experiences and the lens you view them through are the main barriers to living from expectancy. Maybe you are a pragmatist who sees life in a practical way. Maybe you are more of an idealist who believes there is a perfect way to live life. Or maybe you are a champion of intellect whose rationale guides you. Or are you a skeptic who believes idealism is subjective and not verifiable?

These modes of thought are rooted in human experience, and when you view life through these modes the spyglass is narrow. Your capacity to take in new information, to intuit meaning below the surface of objects your five senses filter is largely untapped. As you get older, the lens of your spyglass gets smaller and smaller … sometimes myopic. Your open-mindedness and willingness to learn begins to wane. Why is this?

- Do you have to align with a certain set of values to feel comfortable?

- Are you too tired and indifferent to have a new experience?

- Or ... do you not accept yourself?

The transcendental movement philosophy and thought established by Emanuel Kant and later expanded upon by Ralph Waldo Emerson illustrates this:

> For progress as a true individual under the Transcendentalist way of thought to be possible, self-acceptance is paramount. This could occur only through complete trust in a person's own intuition without influence from outside forces of tradition or religion.

Like his British romantic contemporaries, Ralph Waldo Emerson saw a direct connection between man, nature and God. Historian Grant Wacker describes Emerson's belief:

> God was best understood as a spirit, an ideal, a breath of life; everywhere and always filling the world with the inexhaustible power of the divine presence. God was as close as the atmosphere, as intimate as the blowing clover and the falling rain.

It is no coincidence that I feel most alive and in the posture of awe and wonder than when I am visiting any one of America's national parks. There is no tradition or religion that compares to God's presence being felt in His creation.

Carrie and I have made it a point to expose our children, Isabel and Colton, to our love of the outdoors. It's one of many activities we've chosen to engage in as we continue to change and evolve as the kids get older.

Have you discovered the incredible services the National Park Service makes available to help kids and their families get into parks? A free pass is offered to fourth graders and their families for the entire year. We have taken advantage of this treat with Isabel and then Colton traveling to Yosemite National Park, Sequoia National Park, Arches National Park, Canyonlands National Park, Grand Canyon National Park, Rocky Mountain National Park, Yellowstone National Park, Teton National Park and the Petrified Forest National Park. Every piece of creation has its own WOW factor. It's as though God knew exactly when and how His people were going to experience the treasure of creation.

*Change will not come if we wait for some other person or some other time. We are the ones we've been waiting for. We are the change that we seek.* —Barack Obama

# coach gus' insights

Society and culture do an amazing job of selling you on what you should be and placing ideas, attitudes, and emotions in a compartment, easily labeled, and easily controlled. If you are willing to consult your heart as a source of understanding and wisdom along with your intellect, a new dimension of humanity opens to you. Your strengths become accentuated because you no longer live strictly from your intellect.

# chapter eighteen

# Compartmentalizing Rearrangements

*If everything has a place, and every compartment is filled, is there*
*any room left to change, or your true self to be revealed?*

What would happen if you allowed yourself to speak and
act with a freedom that did not require you to speak
and act differently depending on the people, the place, or the
situation?

If you have found yourself, more often than you would
like to admit, holding your thoughts inside for the fear of
what people will think if you "speak your mind" or feel
you can't be yourself in places and situations, you are
acting from a persona that you have created that stran-
gles your true self from emerging. There is nothing more
frustrating for a man than not to live from his true self,
from the spirit that God gave him. Compartmentalizing
your thoughts, your words, and your behaviors leads to a
suppression of your spirit that is demoralizing. You do not
have to wear a mask any longer!

Rearrangement does not happen without an upheaval. The definition of upheaval is "a violent or sudden change or disruption to something." It is easy to stay put and be comfortable. Comfort and expectancy cannot exist in the same lexicon. You dream big dreams. You see yourself (rightfully so) in a positive and successful light in your relationships, careers, and your life. If you are unhappy, unfulfilled, or unsatisfied, why is that?

Life is fluid and ever changing. What might have given you peace and comfort six months ago may no longer give you that same peace. Take the pandemic that devasted so many. Most everyone has had his or her life affected to some degree.

**Embracing rearrangement can be a game changer for you.**

Rearrangement in this case has come violently and suddenly and is not welcomed, yet it may be necessary. To experience progress and peace during such a time of uncertainty, embracing rearrangement can be a game changer for you. If you use upheaval as an ally and not an excuse, rearrangement can help you live the life you envision. Life changing events lead to life changing actions.

If there is an idea or a passion that has been in your conscience and in your heart, it will find its way to the forefront of your mind. What you do with it from there is the difference between living your dreams and watching them from the screen of your smartphone. The step from having a dream to turning it into reality is smaller than you think. This is why allowing rearrangement to take hold of you is so important to *seizing the day* ... your day.

When a whole new set of ideas, emotions, and attitudes take hold, you start to become sturdy, strong, and full of substance. These new ideas enable you to believe and act on the things that give you purposeful satisfaction. Uncertainty is a true test of how you manage your attitudes, ideas, and changing emotions. Even though these changes are for your good, for you to move closer to your **I have felt what it** dreams, your freedom, the reality you **means to be a phony.** seek, this uncertainty of rearrangement can be scary.

This is why most compartmentalize or segment ideas, thoughts, and attitudes into the role played out in given situations. Whether it's your career, relationships and social circles, you tend to put on a persona of what is acceptable to the situation. The result is you are most likely to be emotionally comfortable.

Compartmentalizing painful emotions and memories can be helpful in the short run and assist you in continuing to operate at productive levels in accordance with your responsibilities. To reach your most productive and integrated self, you cannot mask behind others or yourself. Genevan philosopher, writer, and author of *La Nouvelle Heloise,* Jean-Jacques Rousseau writes,

> The prevalence of masks over actual human faces,
> denouncing the wide-spread pretense in which many
> of his contemporaries complacently reveled.

Masks or personas are the evidence of compartmentalization lived out. For so long, and even at times today, I put on the mask that eases the pressure of feeling uncomfortable in situations where it is difficult to be myself. Along my journey, the greatest motivator has been and will continue to be to align my insides with my outsides. I have felt what it means to be a phony. It is possibly the worst feeling I have ever felt. I fiercely protect and challenge my personality today through reflection and action so that I learn and in some cases unlearn who I am. There is nothing worse or more debilitating than feeling inept. This starts with allowing compartmentalization of thoughts, ideas, and attitudes to go unchecked. At some point you will face yourself, your masks, and your inadequacies. To truly live from your individuated selves as Carl Jung put it,

> Acknowledgment of the inner moral tensions inherent to every individual is essential to rediscover the self and achieve a state of wholeness. Denial of our contradictions and rejection of parts of our psychic experiences only drive us further away from our self, which represents our true identity.

The "inner moral tensions" most experience, in my estimation, is the consciousness of the "source" Kafele. It's Jesus whispering to let His seeds of love, compassion, fullness, boundless grace, grow inside of you.

**Living behind my shadow almost killed me.**

The genesis of this book was inspired by the tension I felt from my role, my desires, and the call to a bold living. I am driven by alignment and acceptance, alignment of my emotions, ideas, and attitudes and acceptance of my contradictions and ego subsets.

Compartmentalization gives you only a partial view of yourself. It delivers the choice to accept what you want to about yourself while leaving thoughts, emotions, and experiences to your subconscious where they can be harmful to your life. Carl

Jung summarizes this difficult but critical moral and psychological task:

> By compartmentalizing, the individual overemphasizes aspects of her/his personality whilst discarding others. As a consequence, (s)he can neither rely on the strengths of an authentic individuality, nor maintain her/his moral and psychological integrity. Awareness of the complexities of self and of the reality of our evil tendencies is morally empowering. By removing the veil behind which we hide our shortcomings, we cease to fear what these might reveal to others and to ourselves, thereby taking charge of our character instead of being led by it.

Living behind my shadow almost killed me. This is why alignment is so important to embrace. By leading out in front of my shadow and allowing Kafele to show me who I am, I can shine so much brighter than the shadows of my pain, my judgments of me. Life changes all the time, seemingly faster as time passes. With change and time come choices. We are all faced with the inevitability of people, places, and things changing to become healthier, to stay relevant, to unveil that bigger, stronger, and faster version.

The choice for you comes in the form of resistance or discovery. The moment you think you cannot grow or experience the newness of life is the moment your attitudes, ideas, and emotions become hard. You were never meant to live with hardness in your heart or a morose sense of being. If you don't have a measure of your discovery and practice a resistance to discovery, your natural inclination is to stay comfortable. The result is that it creates hardness.

> Agency is a fascinating term that encompasses all the self and its ability to act independently from a sense of free will to make decisions. In the process of becoming ... I made a conscious decision for my agency to shine the light of morality, to echo the morality and agency of Jesus Christ. I gave Jesus an all access pass to my thoughts and feelings. That all access pass means breaking down the compartments that I did not know existed. Those compartments deep in my subconscious played an enormous role in my perception of my present circumstances, relationships, and behaviors.

I am driven by authenticity! There may be no worse feeling than saying something, going along with something that does not match what you believe. At that point, you become a robot, programmed with no identity or soul. Compartmentalization of your thoughts and emotions only allows you to process what you tell yourself to. This leaves no room for depth of experience or the connection between your thoughts and emotions.

If you get past the point of compartmentalization, you can open a breadth and depth of experience where life has new meaning. Is it any wonder that authentic connection happens when you are open? Is it any wonder that when you let go of compartments that you designed to protect yourself, you experience healing? Is it any wonder that the weight feels lifted when you break down your compartments?

Psychiatrist Carl Jung viewed "the persona" as the social face an individual presented to the world—a mask—created to make an impression upon others ... concealing the true nature of who the person *really was*. Carl Jung strongly felt that against the surrendering of our individual status to a collective:

...the more individuated a person, the freer the person is to make decisions.

The more a man's life is shaped by the collective norms, the greater is his individual immorality.

The roles you play will drift away in favor of genuine pursuits that give you purpose and passion. Your persona will no longer be important because there is no role to play. A true open partnership with yourself is the source of all life. As Peter compartmentalized his fear and uncertainty seeing Jesus walking on the water calling to him, he broke through his preconceived notion and spoke, maybe the greatest phrase in human history:

> *Lord, if it is you, bid me come to you on the water.*
> —Matthew 14:28

Becoming your individual self and leaving the persona behind takes courage and it takes faith. You can turn Peter's question on yourself: "Self, is it you?" Most play the role and create a persona based on what brings him/her approval and adoration. This starts from an early age. Do you ... did you?

The scariest part of my life was being faced with the notion that I did not know my individual self. That I had spent a lifetime to that point playing roles that were assigned to me. I did not trust the persona that had been created by me and for me. This was an incredibly lonely place for me to discover myself in.

My personal truth revealed: If "myself" is the source apart from persona, I will never be my best self without a moral authority that transcends the self, and the collective. That's heavy for this coach.

Jung's revelation supports where I've landed. He argues that the ultimate purpose of a human life is to achieve individuation, a state of complete transcendence of your dualities and full manifestation of your individuality. How do you do that? Jung continues:

> In order to achieve individuation, one must embark on a quest for self-knowledge, confronting self-deception and accepting the burden of our shortcomings. Compartmentalization prevents self-knowledge by allowing fragmentation of the individual, depriving the individual of the most important source of moral strength one possesses: the self.

As the harsh critic, I have wanted so badly to reject those parts of myself that I do not approve of, or more damning,

**It is time to change.**

my perception of what the world would approve of. "If I could only fit in" was the underlying mantra of my fractured self. The harder I tried, the further away I was from fitting in, and it was destroying me inside. Egos and the subconscious can create amazing illusions: all in the name of "protection."

You and I have a spirit—a life force—that is far stronger, and far more aware than we could possibly know. It is time to change. To turn away from protecting those places you think you need to protect.

- What are the hurts and secrets that you think you should take to your grave?
- What are the disappointments that have lingered from personal and professional relationships that you have put in the closet?

• What are the failures in your life that you live over and over and don't move past?

Turning away from those thick walls you have built within the deeply hidden compartments you have put those memories and feelings in, is difficult to endure. I use the word "endure" because it feels like endurance is the only word that can accurately describe it.

What does endurance mean? The dictionary definition states:

> The fact or power of enduring an unpleasant or complicated process or situation without giving way.

Just like any goal or achievement, there are going to be unpleasant pieces of the journey and difficulties to overcome. You are willing to endure to make money, to seek status, to gain followers, but are you willing to endure to know yourself, to be free mentally, emotionally, and spiritually? Just like building endurance as an athlete, building endurance mentally and emotionally has power—tremendous power. In the physical realm, the power of endurance shows up readily. Mental and emotional endurance may not show up so obviously on the outside, but the power and reassurance of knocking down walls and shining light on compartments is the most powerful journey you will ever take.

You can fake your way into an amazing life—wealth, career, possessions, status—but you cannot fill the hole that exists for genuine connection with those things. I am convinced that you are all looking for genuineness and authentic connection. Is that correct?

When you see it, it is undeniable. Many think you cannot have it because there is something wrong with you. When you grab and embrace these lies, it make the walls thicker, and the compartments move to a darker hiding place. When the walls get thicker and the compartments are harder to find, your resolve to whole heartedly connect with your individual self will fade. In fact, it can evaporate.

The endurance you have built up to weather the emotional storms that come when you are on the journey to your true self starts to weaken. Your persona becomes increasingly attractive. The roles you play become increasingly attractive to live from. The greatest disservice you can ever do to yourself is to settle for comfort over authenticity.

The similarities that you and I share as human beings give us a category of living species on earth. The basic needs and actions we partake in make us similar. These are where the similarities should stop. To stand out from the crowd, you work hard. You persist on building relationships with the person who knows the right person. And you agonize over decades with patience and perseverance to get a shot at the head job, the executive role, the leadership position.

What sets those apart who endure from those who go do something else, or give up altogether?

Is it purpose?

Is it stubborn will?

Or is it something more than this?

Those who stand out find authenticity. They do not let the masses drag them to the sum of collective action and experience. The spirit and fire that flow through them come from the upheaval, the rearrangement, the Hero's Journey. The price to pay is small in comparison to the dividend. The greatest dividend from the tireless and agonizing rearrangement, upheaval, and Hero's Journey is that what it produces will not look the way we thought it would look, which is the true beauty of it all. How many times have you heard from a friend or colleague that they intended to do ABC and ended up with XYZ, and they would not change it for the world. They were willing to be rearranged, to have an upheaval occur, and to go on the Hero's Journey.

If you connect the journey with the source of all life, Kafele, a new dimension of life is opened, one that never ends. All your accomplishments and accolades will seem meaningless when you become a source of strength, substance, and life-giving encouragement. The accolades may come, or they may not. Your accomplishments will build a legacy. Your legacy will endure.

*Endurance is one of the most difficult disciplines, but it is to the one who endures that the final victory comes.*

—Gautama Buddha

## coach gus' insights

You cannot leave with any of your possessions or monetary wealth, but you can leave a wealth of legacy that authenticates the power of your individuality fought for and cultivated over a lifetime.

# 7
# Teaching and Coaching

Start children off in the way they should go, and
even when they are old they will not turn from it.

—Proverbs 22:6

# chapter nineteen

# The Power of a Teacher

*When your experience meets your purpose,*
*teaching and coaching become inevitable.*

Teaching is one of the most undervalued practices, a practice that every person engages in every day. If you really look at your day closely, there will be moments where you are teaching yourself or others to do, to be, to learn something. Yes, you are a teacher … a role model … a mentor. The ability to teach and coach comes from the confidence built over time to believe that you have something to pass on. What you teach is part of *who you are*, the experiences, the thoughts and feelings, the skills learned are all part of your makeup. When your experience meets your purpose, teaching and coaching become inevitable.

If you teach someone something, your integrity takes center stage. Will you teach in a way that equips, that is repeatable, that will allow the student to engage in the precise way he or she engages so they learn best? Teaching and coaching is a multi-faceted, ever changing, highly communicative and relational practice. Everyone has some type of knowledge. Many have been educated at higher learning institutions. And many devour books and take professional development.

But … do you know how to connect and deliver as a teacher and leader? The principles from which you operate works two ways. Either you connect and deliver, or you leave a gap that fails to reach the mark, leaving everyone frustrated.

I've been a teacher and coach for years. There is no worse feeling than being unprepared. As a teacher or coach, you present something all the time. Primarily, you present yourself. Everyone has an initial impression of another when a meeting occurs. Appearance, how you carry yourself physically, the words that you speak, even the tone you use is part of how you present yourself and position to others.

What is heard when you speak generates a myriad of thoughts, questions, emotions, and impressions. All create instant connection or … instant skepticism. People are drawn to the authoritative voice, the one that exudes knowledge and confidence. They are also drawn to the voice that is not afraid to let them see behind the curtain of all that knowledge and confidence, into the fear and doubt. This combination of authority and vulnerability in your speech is connection personified.

**My persona is not who I am.**

When the Holy Spirit was upon me that night in the park, there was an authority and confidence that I spoke with that connected with those kids. Yet, much deeper than that was the care and concern that was exuded in the Holy Spirit coming out of me. At various times, I have struggled with this dynamic of authoritative posture versus the caring and concerning posture.

Can I really command and lead men of any age without an authoritative and ultra-confident persona? It just hit me … my persona is not who I am. It is never who I wanted to be, yet it is who I thought I had to be. The journey to becoming an Oak Tree Source is a relentless pursuit to shedding all the messaging and percep- tions that do not allow you to think, act, and behave from the integration of mind, emotion, body, and spirit. I believe that as teachers and coaches everywhere and unbeknownst in many ways, what is mirrored helps people be themselves. Teachers help give people permission to be themselves.

**Teachers help give people permission to be themselves.**

I am never more myself than when I am teaching, both spontaneous and prepared at the same time. When these two work in tandem, the lesson, the presentation, and the talk take on a quality that creates engagement and connection that are unmatched. The ability as the teacher to stray from the script can be incredibly scary, while at the same time it can be incredibly liberating.

As a student teacher, I had more moments than I would like to admit where I felt ill equipped and embarrassed by the way I managed situations. Spontaneity was the furthest thing from my mind. In my U.S. History class, we were watching an excerpt from a video on the Vietnam War when I could not get the sound to come out of the right speakers. What came out was barely audible. My cooperating teacher had a bull horn in his room. To save the class period and prevent the students from destroying the classroom, instead of trying to fix the speaker, I went off script and put the bull horn in the one speaker that would work to amplify the sound. It didn't.

The whole exercise flopped, and I was left struggling to recover from my ill-conceived makeshift decision. Another time, I was going over an article in class and a student asked a question that I had no answer for. All eyes were on me for the answer. The anxiety and uncertainty were almost unbearable. I stood frozen for what seemed an hour when it was probably only 10 seconds. Teaching requires that teachers have answers. There is not a worse feeling in the world than when you are expected to have an answer and you don't.

Students have technology right at their fingertips in the classroom today. They can fact check their teachers instantly. This scenario goes one of two ways. Teachers can become very insecure and lash out at their classes, or teachers can humble themselves and use the moment as a learning moment for themselves and their students.

My students did this to me my first year at Mullen High School. The honors government class was made up of incredibly smart kids, many of whom were smarter than me—much smarter. Their fact checking became childish after the first few questions they asked. Their objective was to get me in a "gotcha" moment. As a new teacher I was only pages ahead of them when it came to content, which made planning more important. Planning activities where students could enter a collaborative work situation became instrumental in the success of the class. Their collaboration with each other kept me from being in front of them all the time. This allowed them to interact with the content in a way that was beneficial for everyone, including myself. I learned as the students learned.

Every day of my first year at Compassion Road Academy, I walked in with butterflies. I looked forward to getting ready for the day and what it would bring. In my eighth year, I still walk into the classroom with butter-flies each day in expectancy of what the day will bring. With a heart full

**Something meaningful is the teacher's call.**

and hopeful to connect, to transform, to influence, my motivation becomes narrow and clear. The trick is to want to come back and do it again the next day.

I was seriously challenged many days at Compassion Road Academy, coming back each day with the focused motivation to influence, to breakthrough for the students, so the students could experience their own breakthroughs. Whether it was the curiosity to learn something new, or to be loved, I get butterflies in this pursuit because something meaningful is going to happen. That *something meaningful* is the teacher's call. It can be prepared to be drawn out in the mind, catching like wildfire through students' hearts. This is why I keep coming back.

As I write this, schools, students, teachers, and parents are struggling with the ramifications of the pandemic. Education has changed in numerous ways to account for stopping the spread of the virus. The biggest change has been the use of video conferencing, Zoom, Google Meet, etc. While technology has increased so classes can happen, what technology has not done is increase access to the holistic education that occurs when classes meet in person.

St. John Baptist De La Salle, the Patron Saint of teachers, offers this quote that is another reason I keep coming back.

To touch the hearts of your students is the greatest miracle you can perform.

Since the beginning of the pandemic that was birthed in 2019, the CDC reported:

Mental health–related ED visits increased sharply beginning in mid-March 2020 (week 12) and continued into October (week 42) with increases of 24% among children aged 5–11 years and 31% among adolescents aged 12–17 years.

Not to mention depression and suicidal ideation among adults rose sharply during this time. The CDC Data reported:

Overall, 40.9% of 5,470 respondents who completed surveys during June reported an adverse mental or behavioral health condition, including those who reported symptoms of anxiety disorder or depressive disorder (30.9%), those with TSRD symptoms related to COVID-19 (26.3%), those who reported having started or increased substance use to cope with stress or emotions related to COVID-19 (13.3%), and those who reported having seriously considered suicide in the preceding 30 days (10.7%).

At least one adverse mental or behavioral health symptom was reported by more than one-half of respondents who were aged 18–24 years (74.9%) and 25–44 years (51.9%), of Hispanic ethnicity (52.1%), and who held less than a high school diploma (66.2%), as well as those who were essential workers (54.0%), unpaid caregivers for adults (66.6%), and who reported treatment for diagnosed anxiety (72.7%), depression (68.8%), or PTSD (88.0%) at the time of the survey.

Isolation breeds detachment. Your mind is like a super-computer. It can collect, analyze, and magnify every thought that passes through it. In recovery I heard it put this way, "Our minds can be a bad neighborhood to walk through alone." As much connectivity as you may have in the 21st century, most are starving for connection. There is no substitute for presence: none. The energy and substance that your presence brings is undefeated in its ability to nourish souls and spark minds.

*Effective leaders are, first and foremost, good teachers. We're in the education business.*

—John Wooden, American basketball coach

## coach gus' insights

Kids have their entire adult lives to sit in front of a screen and collaborate with professional colleagues. When I have students in the classroom, I maximize that time with substantive connection. Sometimes it's a personal story, sometimes it's an observation in silliness that lightens the mood, or spontaneous songs and whatever comes to mind that has a chance to focus on the essentials: connection, relationship, encouragement and love.

# chapter twenty

# The Classroom
# and the Questions

*You don't have to respect me,*
*but you will respect what happens in this classroom.*

A former student emailed me recently to answer a few questions about teaching as she is starting her foundational education coursework. It is always an honor to have former students think enough of you to ask your advice. The three questions that stood out to me in her survey were:

1. What personality traits or behaviors do you think are essential in teaching?

2. How do you build relationships with your students?

3. How do you balance your authority in the classroom with caring for your students and showing compassion?

My responses to her included:
   *What personality traits or behaviors do you think are*
   *essential in teaching?*

> Speaking the truth in love and *integrity;* having a high energy level that models your *passion* and *purpose*; and a developing social/emotional awareness of people, of humanity that reflects a commitment to relationship building are essential traits. A teacher's behavior must demonstrate having the *courage* to be oneself. Teachers find out a lot about themselves when they become teachers. The best teachers are risk takers, taking risks in strategies, techniques, and what they teach. If your intuition tells you to try something, try it. But know it may totally bomb.

My experience has been that taking risks have been some of the most rewarding in the classroom. It takes all these traits and behaviors to help believe in what I did as a teacher. Once incorporated into how I taught, I can become a model for my students. This is the beauty of teaching. E. E. Cummings put it so well,

> Once we believe in ourselves, we can risk curiosity, wonder, spontaneous delight, or any experience that reveals the human spirit.

They may not know it, but people need to see positive behaviors modeled and in action. The measure of purity you are **Ask questions** willing to exhibit will determine the level of **constantly.** your sincerity. Teaching, by its nature, commands sincerity. Even the false teachers act sincere and believe the stuff they are trying to peddle.

*How do you build relationships with your students?*
This is such a great question. The teacher must be the unquestioned authority in the classroom. The kids must know that

the teacher has their best interests in mind, always. Letting the students have a voice in classroom decisions is a terrific way to build relationships. Social/emotional awareness is a key. Listen to your students' nonverbal communication. There is a lot of it. Ask questions constantly, personal questions, and follow students' activities on school social media. Write personal notes on papers you grade to encourage them.

*How do you balance your authority in the classroom with caring for your students and showing compassion?*
The teacher must have a command/confident presence as well. This means calling out a kid when need be and not wavering from your decision. Many teachers believe you must be strict at the onset and then become more relaxed as the year goes on. This may be the case at the primary levels.

At the high school level, it's different. You trust them first with firm boundaries and great organization and let them demonstrate if they can manage it or not. Work hard to give them meaningful lessons and projects. When you pour your heart out to them, they will appreciate getting to know you. Don't be afraid if a story comes to mind or something relevant apart from the lesson comes up to go down the rabbit hole. They can be so fun and rewarding. Find and bring your sense of humor!

The rabbit hole of awe and wonder that leads to goodness every time is the teacher's ability to share his/her heart.

I recently shared with a class the reason my grandfather would not call me by name. He called me Cowboy. My grandfather Gus lived in Dallas, Texas, and was a Dallas Cowboys fan. My first name came from my great grandfather on my father's mom's side of the family. His name was Julian Britt Hodges. My grandfather would not call me Britt because of disputes that happened long before I was born. Instead, I was "Cowboy" for his love of the Dallas Cowboys and my love of football. I liked my nickname, it suited me well, and became a source of endearment between us.

> Humanizing yourself may be the greatest gift you give those you influence. It is the greatest gift you give yourself. Teachers guard a sacred space and time in kids' lives that can help plant the seeds for future oak trees.

On the first day in class of a new school year, part of my opening script is this statement,

> You don't have to respect me, but you will respect what happens in this classroom.

There have been many young men and women that have come through my classroom's door that have not respected what can happen within the four walls. By the time they leave my class, they have had an experience of learning curriculum. More importantly, they have taken lessons beyond World History or American Government that will be useful to them as they grow into adulthood.

I do social media vlogs as part of my motivational passion and to feed my hunger to speak. They are called *Fired Up Friday* and *Sunday Encouragement.* Fired Up Friday started as a one-off motivational message that turned into an almost every Friday vlog for the last year and a half. The boys at the school where I coach urged me to keep Fired Up Friday going. So, I have, and the boys have loved it, especially during football season.

For my influence to deepen and grow as a teacher and coach, it is a good idea to meet the young people I was called to steward in the places where they may not expect to see me, but they do. If the message is consistent with how I live my life, my influence in the classroom and ball field becomes more authentic. Recently, I had a student pay me a wonderful compliment. She said, "I wish I would have listened more to your stories and scripture talks, you are one of the brightest and full-hearted men I have ever met." This message made my day and was another affirmation of how hungry people are, not just young people, for a message of hope and strength.

Bob Beauprez was a speaker I invited to come to Mullen High School and meet the students. Bob served in the U.S. House of Representatives, was a prominent banker in Colorado, and a true model for the **Confidence can be elusive.** high schoolers as to what it takes to succeed. He spoke about his background and the current state of our government.

His countenance and presence were inspiring to the kids in a way that was bold and illustrated a bar for success that opened the eyes of the students, and for me as well. Bob was teaching all of us through his story that high degrees of achievement like he has accomplished are not only attainable, but they enrich our lives and give us confidence and unapologetic roots that grow strong like an oak tree. Bob Beauprez was one of the best men

I've ever encountered and demonstrated the components of an oak tree!

Confidence can be elusive. If you focus too much on everything going on around you, or compare yourself to others, your confidence can come under fire. It is so important to have the reminders, those people in your life that teach you, and influence you to be yourself. A unique and distinctive you … that is what the world needs. It takes courage to be you, and that courage has never been more personified for me than when I am not self-conscious about the quirks in my personality.

As a follower of Jesus, there are many times when I am walking around the neighborhood, or school, or at the gym, and I'm focusing on my inner self. I will be thinking or praying, and I will hold my hand up in praise of Jesus Christ. Sometimes, my actions create reactions from others. People give me weird looks sometimes, especially in the gym.

I have a silly side that ranges from making faces to speaking in snort and grunts and a quasi-British accent. Carrie always tells friends, and people we meet, that I am the biggest kid in our house. It is true many times. If you can't get your sillies out, is life worth living? I do not eat the hard crunchy ends of French fries, I throw them back on the plate. I burp out sounds like: "eeerrrp" or "rallfff." This has become a running joke in our house.

**Teachers and coaches must be masters of feedback.**

I am not a handy person; I cannot fix much. My belief was that it made me less of a man. I used to drive a Jeep Grand Cherokee that had a diesel engine. We like to travel, and especially road trips. Carrie calls us the Guswolds in reference to the *Vacation* movies starring Chevy Chase. On one trip, I was filling up and put a semi-truck diesel nozzle in the Jeep gas tank. Unbeknownst to me, there are distinct size diesel nozzles. I thought something was wrong when the nozzle did not fit. I hit the trigger and the diesel fuel came flying out, soaking my shoes and pants. That is when I learned there are different size diesel nozzles!

Stinking of diesel fuel, I pulled the Jeep to a regular sized pump. I walked through the median to get a wiper squeegee to wipe the diesel fuel off the side of the Jeep. Capping off the nozzle fiasco, I banged my head on the paper towel dispenser that was attached to the beam above me. It was a comedy of errors to be sure that kept on dominoing. I certainly felt like Clark Griswold in this instance.

I love to sing karaoke. The quickest way to liberate yourself from the feeling of embarrassment is to sing karaoke. Most guys have too much pride to get up in front of others and risk embarrassment. If you never risk looking like a fool, you will never know what it means to be free. You will never know humility if you don't take pride out of the equation. I have been embarrassed many times because I was not humble enough to be teachable and coachable. The ability to be open to feedback and criticism can be the difference between reaching your dreams and attaining significant success and perpetual cycles of offense and blame that lead to a life stuck in neutral.

Teachers and coaches must be masters of feedback. This is where your inner lives must match the words and body language that you express. Everyone expects feedback. It doesn't matter if the feedback is from your closest relationships or the barista at the Starbuck's drive through. Feedback starts with the teacher understanding the students' boundaries mentally, emotionally, and physically so the teacher has an idea what is acceptable and can formulate a style to give feedback.

> Feedback consists of clear, concise communication and timing that builds trust. Many think giving difficult feedback and/or gut level truth is negative. I have had the greatest breakthroughs in my relationships with family, friends, students, players, and coaches when difficult truths are brought up. There is no time to patronize people, especially when you are working toward a common goal.

Timing may be the most important aspect of giving and receiving feedback. As a teacher and coach, feedback happens many times in the moment. Coaching feedback, particularly in football, has consisted of coaches yelling at their players.

**You must learn to communicate in someone else's world.** Although it is descriptive, this form of communication struggles to connect and build trust on meaningful levels. As much as kids today don't know, and are no different than kids of previous generations, they now have access to information at a level that has never been seen in human history.

Trust me, I have seen some bone-headed behavior as a teacher and coach. With that said, kids know more, and they want to be treated like they do. Does this mean their emotional maturity is on par with someone of professional stature? Of course not. The gap between intellect and emotional maturity is widening for young people. They are filled with information but do not connect that information to their hearts. This is the gap teachers and coaches can and must pour their knowledge and experiences into.

Teaching and coaching in the modern context commands connection before content. The first day of school or practice goes a long way in shaping the message and method the teacher and coach intends to lead with. In *Everyone Communicates, Few Connect*, author John Maxwell reveals,

> If you want to get your message across, you must learn to communicate in someone else's world.

> The best teachers and coaches know this, and they learn how to create a world of passion, preparation, performance, and purpose that focus on the students and athletes.

Creating a world for those you teach and coach does not mean you are a doormat for their desires, opinions, likes and dislikes. What it means is that you are the source for their new knowledge. You are the starting point that lays the groundwork for connection, the experience, the growth, physically, mentally, emotionally, and spiritually. Stepping into their world means stepping out of yours. This is where influence really begins. This means seeing, hearing, being aware of those clues your students give you and anticipating what they need, at precisely the right time that they need it.

More times than I can count, I have looked out over a classroom and/or team that seemed disinterested. My teaching side would tell me that it was the time to shake up the agenda by taking a risk. Create an impromptu debate in class, with the topic chosen by the students. Or, let a 5-8 minute bell ringer activity go 45-48 minutes because students were engaged and were connecting on levels they may not have previously. Take a risk ... and see what happens.

Teachers and coaches can never forget that they signed up to influence first and reap rewards that they may never see. We, and you, are called to be sturdy like an oak tree. Combining that sturdiness of character, attitude, and action with the conscious decision to be a source of these things for those you teach and coach, purposeful satisfaction is enough.

One testimony of what it means to be an Oak Tree Source stands out for me. Dominic Depizzol was one of my former players and the quarterback for Mullen High School at the time. I shared many great victories and significant challenges in the three years we were together, allowing us to develop strong roots of common purpose and respect for each other. He is one of the finest young men I know and is creating his own legacy as an Oak Tree Source. Dom discovered that I was applying for a head coaching position at another school. He volunteered to write a letter of recommendation in support of me:

> To Whomever It May Concern,
> I have had the privilege of knowing and being coached by Britt Gusmus for three years. You will not find a man anywhere who more genuinely cares for his players on, and most importantly, off the field. In my experience, he has been much more than a football coach. He is in the profession of molding his players into honorable and respectable young men. As a leader and someone all his players looked up to, he never let outside distractions get in the way of his interactions with us. I can remember multiple times when he was struggling with an ill family member, and he came to

practice regardless with a great attitude and charisma that radiated to all of us.

His interactions with us would instill a sense of confidence that we may have not had before just by the way he carried himself. Not once did he ever turn someone away if they wanted to talk; he always took ample time to talk to everyone he crossed paths with. His profound love of God and of his family gave order to what he did for us on the football field as he knew there was something more important to what was going on in our lives.

As a football coach, you trusted greatly his opinion because of his vast athletic background and the experiences he has had along the way. He garners respect among his players not because he demands it, but because he deserves it. He is a relentless learner and was always forming new ways to add in a drill or learn a new technique to show us when practice came. In the three years I've known him on the football field, he's coached everything from quarterbacks to tight ends to running backs. He's never sulked but took each opportunity to make his position unit the best on the team.

I may be biased. Coach Gusmus is a man I greatly admire; one who has changed my life greatly not only because of what he told me on the football field but more importantly, because of what he told me off the field. I can assure you he will carry himself with the dignity and respect to change the culture of any program and make a difference in the lives of those within it.

The impact teaching and coaching make on people's lives cannot be overstated. When a copy of my player's letter was sent to me, I was humbled ... and honored. It is not all about teaching curriculum and coaching scheme, while these are both essential to success, the work that creates the fertile ground is *knowing*.

- Knowing when to push and knowing when to ease up when delivering content and scheme.

- Knowing when to break from it all and feed them where their lives are. This takes observation, conversations, experience, and trust for your students and players.

- Knowing them means the more you walk toward them, they will buy-in more; give more sacrifice; and trust more in what you the teacher and you the coach are trying to build.

- Knowing their hearts, above all.

The game of football does an excellent job of revealing what is inside of the player. Every meeting, every practice, every interaction says something about the level of commitment. Can coaches instill strength and resolve? No. But they can create the environment where these traits are on display. The players can then decide as to whether they want to strive for that themselves or not.

Teachers and coaches need to put the mirror up for students and players every day. The mirror gives evaluation not only of performance progress but of attitudes, thoughts, and connections being made or not. Notre Dame's legendary football coach Knute Rockne said,

> The secret is to work less as individuals and more as a team. As a coach, I play not my eleven best but my best eleven.

If you want to be one of the best eleven, you will allow the mirror to change you. Teachers and coaches who focus on "team" and/or "community" first and always, will reap what they have sewn. The harvest is abundant with inspiration, motivation, common purpose, and genuine care and concern for the person next to them.

Care and concern are the underrated qualities that make up great teaching and coaching. Showing care and concern starts with serving. My first day at my first school, our entire staff cooked pancakes, bacon, and eggs for the students and families who could attend. Our community was small at the time but for some, it may have been the only hot meal they would get that day and have warm and concerned interactions with others.

My story would be incomplete, and would not have substance, if I did not come to the jumping off point and take the risk to become a teacher and a coach. Once it became clear to me that my **Taking risks is where connection lies.** story was worth something, and worth telling, risks become a little easier to take.

Recently, a student came to me in Forensic Law class and asked, "Why do drug courts and those incarcerated for drug crimes not get more help from the justice system to be rehabilitated?" It's a superb question.

I have direct experience with recovery and working with transitional programs for addicts coming out of the prison system. I took the risk. I revealed to tell her that I was 15 years sober, and that I have spoken at and worked with organizations that help those transitioning back to life and staying sober.

Taking risks is where connection lies. In a time where we are isolated more now than ever, helping people of all ages plant acorns that will grow is as important as it's ever been. I took a risk just recently as I walked by a man while walking our dog. I have walked by this man before, and he has had a scowl on his face each time. This time, we exchanged "Hellos" as we passed each other. Then I turned back and asked, "Is there something I can pray about for you?" His eyes opened as if I was an alien. He opened up about the troubles he was having in his life, and we talked ... we connected. I cared and he appreciated it.

Small risks like that make a significant difference. I hope I have planted an acorn in that man's life. The risk/reward quotient is multiplied when lives are impacted in tangible ways. I receive letters from students at various times during the school year. This is not only the reward I receive when I read their heartfelt words about genuinely being impacted by our time together. What gets me excited is when I see the impact they make in their own lives and the lives of others. One wrote:

Thank you for everything you've done for me and our school. You have had the greatest impact on me as a student.

I really appreciate how you are always excited to teach and make the day of learning the best it can be, no matter the circumstances.

You have such a positive outlook on things is what I like most about you. No day is a bad day for you, just less exciting than usual. I know I can always count on you for advice or someone I know I can come to for a welcome smile. You always make us feel safe and appreciated, which sends us kids going home with a reason to come back.

Thank you again for all the wonderful work you have done for our community and our education, the least I can do is say … thank you.

This is multiplication. Jesus understood this and gave us the model in the Gospel of John:

> *You did not choose me, but I chose you and appointed you so that you may go out and bear fruit, fruit that will last and so whatever you ask in my name the Father will give you.*
> — John 15:16

The concept of multiplication is a key component to growing unshakeable roots of influence, encouragement, love, and passion. One of the greatest ways to build these essential traits is to teach and coach. Whether you know it or not, you are teaching and coaching every day in every interaction you have.

*To be as good as it can be, a team must buy into what you as the coach are doing. They must feel you're a part of them and they're a part of you.*    —Bobby Knight

# coach gus' insights

An act of spontaneity, being the mirror, taking risks, multiplying by appreciating and helping others feel safe are all life-giving, purposefully satisfying acts that build strength and substance that help you become sturdy like an oak tree.

# 8 A Sturdy Oak

They will be called oaks of righteousness, a planting of the Lord for the display of his splendor.

—Isaiah 61:3

# chapter twenty-one

# The Signs Spoke Loudly

*For some odd and morbid reasons,*
*humanity, it seems, likes destruction*
*more than purity and peace.*

I never intended to be a "planting of the Lord." I never intended to be righteous. I always thought of myself as strong, passionate, and someone who was cool with a unique sense of charisma. I fought so hard to find my individuality because those traits I mentioned were not planted on firm ground that would last. Unworthiness was my calling card; looking for sympathy was my way to get attention. Then I jumped into the unknown, and my story began.

There was a janitor at one of the schools I worked at who loved to talk. Most of the time he wanted to talk about sports. I was happy to oblige. In many of our conversations, it felt to me that these may be some of the only conversations this man had during the day. We talked football from many different angles, from individual players, to teams, to college football, and the NFL draft. The passion this man had for football would make any coach or football historian proud. I was fertile ground. I was a starting point for this man to let his passion flow.

The acorns that you spread may not grow into sturdy oak trees, but they can be a source of strength and substance that shows others that there is fertile ground to be heard, to be noticed, to be valued.

My story continues to be as though I am "tracing a call back to its source." In many action movies and spy movies, call tracing is used to find the protagonist who most of the time is being chased by bad guys disguised as good guys or for literary purposes, the antagonist. Every call I've made, every loud roar, every tear, every scream of frustration and disappointment I've made, I've been led back to the source of all life. The journey to writing *The Oak Tree Source* and becoming sturdy like an oak tree could have never happened without tracing the call back to Him. Presently, tracing the call God placed on my life back to Him has been difficult. For some reason, He has seemingly been silent.

At the time of this writing, I have just had my eighth interview to be a head high school football coach at a competitive school. These last three years, it has felt like the source has vanished. I am out here on my own calling and no one picks

**It is not about me ....
It's not just about us.**

up. I am still waiting to hear if I move onto the next round of interviews. There have been little nudges along the way. While listening to Dallas Willard's audiobook *Life Without Lack* when he was speaking about "agape love," in that moment I noticed a Gutter Company truck parked across the street. The name of the company was Agape Gutters. When nudges occur, the roots of my presence and character grow deeper and stronger. My intention is to create more fertile ground so that there would be more plantings of the Lord. In Mark, Jesus gives a parable about a sower and the different types of soils on which he scattered seeds:

> *Then he told them many things in parables, saying:*
> *A farmer went out to sow his seed. As he was scattering*
> *the seed, some fell along the path, and the birds came and*
> *ate it up. Some fell on rocky places, where it did not have*
> *much soil. It sprang up quickly because the soil was*
> *shallow. But when the sun came up, the plants were*
> *scorched, and they withered because they had no root. Other*
> *seed fell among thorns, which grew up and choked the*
> *plants. Still other seed fell on good soil, where it produced*
> *a crop—a hundred, sixty or thirty times what was sown.*
> *Whoever has ears, let them hear.*
>
> —Mark 4: 3-9

I listened and my seed planting continued.

As much as I want to see men all over the world grow their presence and character into sturdy oak trees, many will not have ears to hear, or their soil may have distractions, and obstacles in the way. Every time I look at myself under the Tree of Life in New Orleans, I am reminded of how much more I can be, how far and wide my impact on this world can be. And how much more you can be and the potential impact you can have. Have you thought about it?

Lean into and grasp the words, "It is not about me. It's not just about us." The greatest seasons of growth in my life have been when my focus is on planting acorns of love, encouragement, and service to those around me. There was a man I used to help in the rooms of recovery. Actually, we helped each other. As we sat in meetings, I poured encouragement and love into him, and we would get dinner sometimes afterward. One night, I had brought food to his home. He was not well—emotionally, mentally, or spiritually. I asked him if I could pray for him, and I laid a hand on him and started praying audibly. After that night, I did not see him for quite a while. I heard that he stayed sober for the longest length of time he ever had. Whether it had anything to do with me praying for him, I will never know, yet, if we are willing to be used and not make it about us, amazing things seem to always happen. There have been many times that I have fought myself in reaching out to people and breaking through the walls that say *It is about me, it's all about me.*

The Christian Music Festival, Heaven Fest, was always an amazing day of music and worship held in Colorado for many years. The festival took an interesting turn one year when I asked one person if I could pray for him and ended up praying with many more people that day. A couple came walking up to me with their daughter and said, "We heard you pray for people. Will you please pray over our daughter?" I was humbled in a way that I have rarely experienced.

I was turning into a righteous oak. I felt it sprouting within me. The word righteous as defined biblically reveals:

Acting in accord with divine or moral law, being free from guilt or sin, morally right or justifiable.

Throughout these pages, I have spoken of purity. The older I get and the more I mature, this concept becomes more important. I know that I can't grow in wisdom without moving closer and closer to purity in heart and mind. Few are aware of how destructive they can be with themselves and others until they are shown another way.

For some odd and morbid reasons, humanity, it seems, likes destruction more than purity and peace. Prevailing thought indicates that power leads to destruction and corruption. World history in many cases has proven this thought right. Musician and guitarist Jimi Hendrix puts the idea of how we should view power well, when he stated,

**It was something I could not produce in and of myself.**

> *When the power of love overcomes the love of power, the world will know peace.*

It takes a conscious decision to defer power in the name of love. The substance of becoming a righteous oak is built on the idea of giving power away in the most powerful way. That most powerful way is letting the God of the Universe grow you into a righteous oak. As a man, if you fear losing or giving away power, then you'll always have power struggles with people, places, and things. As I walked into the park the night I was baptized in the Holy Spirit, I felt like I was 10 feet tall, even into the next morning as I went to a meeting of Alcoholics Anonymous.

I was helpless to reproduce the amazing 10-foot-tall feeling myself. I could not even compare the feeling to the exhilaration of my wedding day, or college graduation, or winning a state championship, or getting the telegram that I had been drafted by a professional baseball team, or the birth of our children. Nothing could reproduce what the source of all life produced in me that evening.

> If there was ever a mountain top feeling of strength, substance, and personal satisfaction that was it for me. I thought I was a sturdy oak tree. That feeling has been validated with those seminal moments in my life. Feelings do not last, and they can lead you astray if you let them. When you are in command of your mind, body, soul, and spirit, experiences can be the acorns that grow into strong roots. The roots that will flourish and grow into an individual of character. You ... your presence is sturdy like an oak tree.

I was part of a committee that assisted in evaluating school culture. Its focus was on the relationships, interactions, beliefs, core values, and mission and how we were living those out. For me, it was a great experience as I worked with three dedicated and loving colleagues that I admired. For a positive culture to build at our school, there must be connection and community. Our committee put together events that were worthy of both.

One event included a game show designed to highlight individual faculty. As the game show host, I called teachers out of the stands and asked them questions. But more importantly, I spoke about the life of each person who came up through stories of who they are. There was something shared personally and/or professionally about each person who was featured so all knew about their colleagues and their unique and special values and achievements inside and outside of the classroom. There also were questions that spoke to the great history of the school and the events that made the school what it is today. It was an impactful day for everyone and well appreciated.

My years and experiences reveal that I am doing exactly what I was made to do in situations like this, whether it is in the company of one or ten thousand ... pouring, knowing, calling forward the goodness and authenticity of people by any means necessary. When I do this ... when you do this, three things happen:

- Acorns are planted.

- Roots are set deeper.

- Essential stuff is created, not only in you, but in others.

There are seasons in your life, or possibly your entire life where you can't hear, see, or feel your worth and value. I firmly believe you need people to remind you, to show you the signs and wonders of who you are. The apostles of the early Christian church bathed in the Holy Spirit after Jesus ascended to Heaven, preached the word of God.

In 2 Corinthians 12:12, the apostle Paul said this as encouragement and exhortation of the church. "The signs of a true apostle were performed among you with utmost patience, with signs and wonders and mighty works."

The signs and wonders that have pointed to this book have been nothing short of amazing. In 2017, Carrie bought me two journals, both with beautiful **A memory quickly** leather bound covers, one with a quote **dropped in.** from Martin Luther King and the other from Edmund Lee. Carrie suggested I start journaling to remove the power from negative thoughts I might have. As I started writing, I was reminded of another conversation I had with a friend a few years ago, where she recommended I write a book. As that decision became clearer, Carrie gave me more input in terms of our dynamic as husband and wife—commitment as a team.

The next sign came from a conversation with the pastor of our church, who, upon hearing the idea for this book, mentioned the name Kafele for Jesus and what that meant. The concept and title started to really come together as I jogged one day and asked God for guidance. A memory quickly dropped in. The Holy Spirit helped me recall a time of prophecy ... that I would grow into a strong oak tree.

The loudest sign came right before the COVID-19 virus shut down the country. I was at coffee with three former students, when a man approached me, revealing his story and the book he wrote. He reminded the four of us to "tell our stories."

The clarion call was in. It felt like God was speaking directly to me, repeatedly, when my 10-year-old daughter asked, "When is your book going to be finished?" The wonder and purity of her question had me telling myself ... *If this is not a sign, then I'm not sure what is.*

*If you're going to have a story, have a big story, or*
*none at all.* —Joseph Campbell

# coach gus' insights

Your story is more valuable than you know. When
you let the God of the Universe be your guide, you
will start to see the signs and wonders of who you
are and the impact you can make.

# chapter twenty-two

# It's About You
# ... and Us

*When you stand for others and provide a presence
of protection, reliability, responsiveness, and sturdiness,
it gives them the space they need to blossom.*

We all need to hear something that we can trace to a source of goodness, whether it be inside of us, or the source of all life, God. I do. You do. In the biblical context, signs and wonders meant everything from driving out evil spirits to raising people from the dead, to giving His son and daughters messages He wants them to share. The Apostle Paul went on to be specific about gifts given to believers. He states:

> *Having gifts that differ according to the grace given to us, let us use them: if prophecy, in proportion to our faith; if service, in our serving; the one who teaches, in his teaching; the one who exhorts, in his exhortation; the one who contributes, in generosity; the one who leads, with zeal; the one who does acts of mercy, with cheerfulness.*
>
> —Romans 12: 6-8

You have things you do well, whether born with natural gifts or skills you have worked incredibly hard to develop on your own. I am always fascinated by people using their gifts and skills with passion and zeal. As a person who has experienced natural giftings in athletics and the exhilaration they manifest, none of those have come close to stepping into the gifts of the Spirit.

To see people come alive, for their soul to be on fire, nothing, I mean nothing, is more important than that. What can you do to help others step into their spiritual giftings? Start with:

- You can believe in them.

- You can go before them and show them a path.

- You can be a foundation.

All are starting points and leave a trail of acorns that point to the one that will help them find their gifts: God.

Pouring life-giving encouragement into others is a personal mission of magnitude. If you want the impact to have lasting effect, there are three ways you can go about it.

1. **Listen.** It's first and foremost. Listen with your ears for the substance that people are calling for and/or needing strength for in their lives. Maybe it's a relationship, a job, a difficult season in their lives. When you listen to encourage, you will hear what you need to hear.

2. **See.** The things that people don't say audibly tell volumes about what is going on with them. Learn to see with the eyes of the Spirit.

**3. Encourage.** Become a source of substance and strength for them. It's courageous and pays your encouragement forward.

When you stand for others and provide a presence of protection, reliability, responsiveness, and sturdiness, it gives them the space they need to blossom.

- ✓ Interactions can be in a moment, or over long periods of time.

- ✓ Interactions can be acting as a game show host and showing people that they are appreciated ... a celebration of them, not you.

- ✓ Interactions can be taking that prompting of the Spirit and asking or sharing what was given to you with others.

> The things you can do to encourage are endless when you listen and see with the eyes of your heart. Then act by pouring out encouragement and expecting nothing in return.

If growing toward righteousness is the price I must pay to let my roots grow strong and deep, so that I can be a source of life-giving encouragement, strength, and substance for all those I encounter, it will be with honor. John Bevere makes a strong point when he states, "True honor is an outflow from a heart that fears God."

Another word for fear used in the context of God is reverence. I revere life and the human spirit, and through my experiences, I came to revere God. Through reverence, and seeing honor modeled for me as a boy by my mother, I continue growing toward righteousness.

I watched her honor my father as a wonderful wife and partner. Dinner was always on the table, she acted with exuberance to see her husband come through the door after work. Her energy and zest for life have always inspired me. Her traditional values have rubbed off on me. She brought these values into marriage with a purity and ideal that was honorable.

Mom taught my brother and me manners, not only to say "please" and "thank you," but a way of life rooted in family and honoring family first. She was the original oak tree. Her father, my grandfather, was a tremendous influence in what it means to honor others and be honorable. Grandpa honored his family and lay down his life for them every day. Mom did the same for her two sons.

She was the one constant in my life when I was younger, the sturdy oak that I could lean on when everything fell apart. In a world that pounces quickly to put people down, those that have a heart set toward honoring others are truly a planting of the Lord. Mom was not silent. She used to yell so loud and with such conviction at my games that even in a crowd of thousands of fans, I thought I could hear her as I was going to take the next snap in a football game.

If you are to become sturdy like an oak tree, it is of paramount importance that you find ways to honor others. That includes yelling as loud as you can in some way until the whole world hears honor flowing.

God honors our desires, hopes, and dreams. He certainly did when he brought Carrie into my life. I honored her with this poem I wrote to honor her.

# Carrie

*You heard my cries, my pleas, my groans.*
*You prayed for me in my time of heartache.*
*You showed me the purity in her radiant soul.*

*She is out there being molded and shaped for you.*

*But I'm not worthy of such beauty and glory ...*
*Yet, my hope lies in your words and promises.*

*God, you fill me with purpose and meaning and the love*
*I've always searched for.*

*Your presence is all I want.*
*Your presence is all I need.*

*My son, my beloved son, I am proud of you.*
*You bring me great joy.*

*The keys to the Kingdom are yours.*

*The one I have saved for you is being shaped and molded*
*right now.*

*With elegance, beauty, and magnificence her presence will*
*illuminate your path.*

*Praise the Lord, his glory has been placed upon us.*

*I shout the name "Carrie" from every mountain top and the*
*Lord agrees.*

*You showed the love you have for me in bringing me the one that*
*loves you*

*She is right in front of you, made in my image, worth dying for.*

*Take care of her, my son.*

The greatest honor that has ever been bestowed upon me was being saved by the grace of a good God who loves me and knows me better than I do myself. That same God has given me the greatest desire of my heart, which was to enter matrimony with the one he saved for me, Carrie Dianne Gusmus. After 12 years, with strong conviction, I can say that God chose us for each other as a display of his splendor. I

**If you are willing to be changed, the best things in life will happen.**

am never more myself than when I am honoring Carrie and my children, Isabel and Colton.

When people see honor in action, they cannot help but be attracted to it and curious about it. In becoming a righteous oak, worthy of His splendor, it doesn't always look the way you think it should look. If it needs to look a certain way, you are living from the *letter of the law* as opposed to the *spirit of the law*.

> The *letter of the law* tells you that traditional roles cannot be changed.

> The *spirit of the law* tells you to shine. You've got to be a laydown light for them.

The letter of the law always keeps you from purposeful satisfaction. When I chose a strong, accomplished, passionate, and loving woman to be my partner, the compartments I placed pride, position, and authority in were going to come down or I would be on my own. I had to change.

Just as the oak tree grows over time, my walls came down over time as well. For the flow of growth to continue, you cannot be bound by the way things ought to be. I have heard so many stories of friends, others that I know. Stories with words that reflect: "I started down this road and before I knew it, things changed completely." If you are willing to be changed, the best things in life will happen.

Who leads the leaders? For every person leading in whatever capacity, there are those at the foundation, sources of wisdom and knowledge, listening ears, and a presence that is safe. These are the righteous oaks. In many ways, I have and continue to be one of these people. The profession of teaching and coaching is inherently in the position to lead leaders.

I love being the listening ear and safe presence for Carrie. She started her business a few years ago; one that is doing well. Sometimes, she comes home and needs a safe and sturdy presence, not to give advice, as much as I want to at times, but to know that I am with her and know that there is an alert and listening ear right beside her.

Most nights, I tell Bel and Colt stories about my life as a kid growing up. It is life-giving for all of us. I want them to know everything about me. Yes, the good ... but it was much of the turmoil and chaos that brought me to where I am today. Many of those stories will be shared when they are a little older.

Telling stories to them is a lot like tracing calls back to their source. Since Carrie and I are their parents, we are their earthly source. If they get a glimpse of who they are, and who they can be from knowing where I came from, the righteous oak is taking deeper root. When I say, "I love you, Bel," as I leave the room, she says, "Thank you." She doesn't know it yet, but I feel so honored by that thank you. I want her to always feel that she is loved and honored. Honor knows no limits. Its encouraging and enduring qualities can change lives.

Francesca Battistelli has a lyric in her song "Defender" that moves me every time I hear it. It opens with *When I thought I lost me* ... and closes with ... *Put me back together.*

God has always known where I have left me. I've been standing on the roots of His love, but sometimes I just haven't known it. *Do you know where you have left you?* If you build

**Do you know where you have left you?**

your life on the roots of the starting point, the generative force Kafele and the substance and strength that creates, you will always know where you leave yourself planted, righteous and for His splendor.

Becoming an Oak Tree Source would not be complete without a fierceness and resolve that gets tested all the time. I gave a talk before one of our games—the first talk I ever gave before a game. The topic was based on Benaiah the warrior during Biblical times who served under David and Solomon.

I started my talk with two citations from scripture. Below is my short talk:

## In the Pit with a Lion on a Snowy Day

*And Benaiah the son of Jehoiada, the son of a valiant man, of Kabzeel, who had done many acts, he slew two lion like men of Moab: he went down also and slew a lion in the middle of a pit in time of snow.*

—Benaiah 2 Samuel 23:20-23

*He was in greater honor than any of the Thirty, but he was not included among the Three. And David put him in charge of his bodyguard.*

—1 Chronicles 11:25

Benaiah was one of the thirty: David's mighty men.

These were not your everyday soldiers; these were elite soldiers in Moab.

And, these were BATTLES … not a scuffle, not playing patty cake, as we do sometimes when we are blocking. These were dog fights. They were bloody and nasty and activated the fight, flight or freeze response. At that moment, it was kill or be killed. By sheer will and force, Benaiah slayed these men.

As for the pit, with the lion, on a snowy day.

Let's put this event in context. In the winter cold season and snow, lions are fiercer because they are in need of prey and their appetite is much sharper in cold seasons because prey is not as abundant. With that in mind, can you imagine the fight that ensued with Benaiah and this fierce lion?

Again, he found himself in a kill or be killed situation. Through valiance—the brave, bold, assertive, fearless, courageous, and resolute that carried him—and with a sense of honor, Benaiah claimed victory in that pit on that snowy day.

Men, each of you will face your own pit moment(s) on a snowy day with a fierce and hungry lion. In those moments, you will find out about your courage, resolve, bravery, and ability to be bold.

And you will have choices to make. Are you going to end this night held in honor and valiance by your teammates; by your coaches; by your classmates; faculty and community who are going to be watching tonight? Or will you freeze? Or will you run away from the battle? Or when you can finish them, will you take it?

Are you willing to take your opponent's spear and kill him with it? Will you be up to the challenge of exercising your Will with speed, force, agility and intellect to claim victory and take your place among the trusted, valiant, and honorable members of this team?

Last week, we made our opponents die for their cause. They lost; we won. And we played with honor and valiance in respect for our opponents.

This week, you must take the victory from them. When they are down, you cannot be afraid to finish them. Like that lion in the pit, who was fiercely looking for prey, your opponents tonight will be looking for you and when you see it in their eyes, that you are the ones who are the killers.

Will you be bold enough to finish them?

> Will it be said of you by that man next to you tonight that you played with fire, ferocity, and fearlessness? *I am honored to have played next to you tonight.*
>
> If you can look at that man next to you and say what I just mentioned; we will be victorious.
>
> *I am honored to have played next to you tonight.*

When you find yourself in a cold season, relying on the roots you've established through acting your way into righteousness and relying on what God has planted in you, you create a fierceness that cannot be taken away. An inevitable part of life is exercising your will. In the game of football, moving people against their will and tackling them against their will are all difficult to accomplish. It takes all your focus, your strength, your intellect, and the man next to you to use his will in the game of football to its greatest usefulness.

Much like the protective covering the oak tree produces, tannin, a football team acts much like tannin does. The team's ability to protect its own and bring out the color and richness of each member is nothing short of amazing. On that night in Washington state during the game that I gave my talk included above, the acorn of fierceness was planted in one of my players the season before. I was a running back coach at this point in my coaching career. The young man I am speaking of was a junior and had sat behind two seniors throughout his high school career. We were in a league game, and our senior had just broke a long run and needed a breather. I subbed in the less experienced player and on his first carry, he fumbled the ball and turned it over.

Our head coach got into my personal space and just stared at me for what seemed to be 10 minutes. The younger player's confidence took a big hit because he had wanted to show what he could do. The next week, the same situation happened with the senior player, and I put him back in. This time our head coach said, "If he fumbles again, you two are leaving." Just as those words were coming out of his mouth, my sub player took a handoff for a forty yard splint and almost scored. An acorn was planted that day.

Fast forward to the next year to Washington state once again. My junior was now a senior and was playing at an extremely high level. On this night, with confidence brimming, he would rush for over 200 yards and two touchdowns almost leading us to victory. We lost 31-28. What came out of that game was a young man, roots deepening and a righteous oak growing. A couple months after the season, I received a message from his mom that read,

> I want to tell you how much I appreciate you seeing the special in my son. The words you said about him at the football banquet were heartfelt and moved me to tears because you understood his heart, tenacity, and dedication to football despite the doubt and negativity that surrounded him throughout his career at Mullen. You helped him surpass it all and more importantly believed in him when so many doubted. You were a vital person in his life during those years.

I thank you for all you did for my son. Of course, he is a special kid to me but you also took the time to see the light in him for things beyond football. Thankfully, he is doing well at Creighton and we are so proud of him.

So, thank you for being a great teacher, mentor, and coach. I am eternally grateful.

Being an Oak Tree Source means you not only see the *special* in people, but you actively look for it, build your awareness of it, so that you can help them call it forward in their own lives. And, when they need reminding, you remind them of who they are. I am so thankful to have had the time I did with that young running back who taught me about what determination and perseverance means on a deeper level.

In the spring of 2018, I started an exercise in my classes called Motivation Mondays. One student would choose a video, a phrase, reading, or something that motivated him. I would take the theme and speak life into the students. The kids loved it, and it was another way for me to call forward a relentless positive message for them to think about and reflect on. A student played *The Pale Blue Dot,* a video based on Carl Sagan's speech. The combination of the video and the speech narration was powerful. As the camera transitions from the earth into our solar system and ultimately the universe, and views the earth once more, it looks like a pale blue dot in the mind-blowing vastness of outer space.

As I watched, my hurts and hang ups seemed so insignificant and the devastation that humanity has perpetrated on itself for much of human history seemed so silly and confusing as to why so much seems to be in chaos and confusion. Perspective is such a powerful tool. If you believe you are a victim, your perspective will search for those instances to validate your thoughts. If you believe your best is yet to come, the same validation principle applies. When pouring positive perspective out through any channel, the result is a product of the energy and exuberance you receive from your roots being nourished on the firm foundation of the God of the Universe.

As I put the final touch on my words, disturbing data were released by the CDC on life expectancy. It's declined more than a full year for Americans, dropping to 77.3 years from 78.8 pre COVID. The drop off is the sharpest since World War II. Not only is the virus taking lives, but the effects of isolation and hopelessness are taking lives as well. The message of the Oak Tree Source could not be more important than it is today. The Apostle Paul gives this statement that is timeless in its wisdom, yet, seemingly so hard to practice for humanity.

> *Let your conversation be always full of grace,*
> *seasoned with salt, so that you may know*
> *how to answer everyone.*
> —Colossians 4:6

If you approached every conversation and encouragement through Paul's lens, I believe people would come out of isolation and feel a permeating hope that is tangible and meaningful. It is not idealistic or naive to think that gracefully considering others in your thoughts, actions, and words could change the world. You could also think of salt and flavor as your personal currency. Ask yourself the question while looking through the lens of Colossians 4:6.

How much grace and consideration do you have for others?

This is your currency. With lives being lost, investing in your heart currency instead of monetary currency creates a yield spread that value cannot be placed because one is so much more valuable than the other.

*Who sows virtue reaps honor.* —Leonardo da Vinci

## coach gus' insights

Being in the spotlight—the center of attention—the leading man or woman is not nearly as gratifying as being the laydown light, the source for others. Your presence and impact will grow exponentially when you make it about others, and not yourself.

# chapter twenty-three

# My Final Thoughts

*The weight I carry in day-to-day life*
*seems heavy at times and I'm not inspired.*

Astrange phenomenon happens when heart currency
develops in you. You start to anticipate where you can be
graceful and considerate toward others. The Holy Spirit starts
to guide your thoughts, and you can assess and evaluate what
needs people have and act to help. Just like the oak tree is a
provider for multiple organisms, you can be dependable, consistent, and sturdy for others in ways they never know when
you enter a partnership with the Holy Spirit. There is freedom
in this partnership that you have never known. Not only do
you become bound by your emotions, thoughts, and influences,
but they stay in your body affecting your physical health.

In a dream, I got a glimpse of life lived without being
bound by my emotions, thoughts, and influences. My first
reaction was, "Oooh, I'm free," with a surprised thought, as
I walked toward what seemed to be smoke. The comfort,
ease, and pure but forceful weight in my spirit was the most

freeing experience I have encountered. There was no more anxiety, fear, stress, or worry.

> The weight I carry in my day-to-day life seems heavy at times and I can become uninspired. Becoming a sturdy oak tree in attitude, thought, and action helps me carry the weight that I may never be able to shed, not in this life, anyway. As it will you. It is certainly easy and many think justified to grab self-righteous anger and judgment. It becomes intoxicating to point the finger and gather others' support for the ways you have been wronged and harmed, and life is not going your way. I've experienced this feeling.

All these emotions stay trapped in your body, mind, and spirit. If you don't process them and gain perspective, you start to live with regret that leads to staying stuck in your same patterns and processes. Ultimately, your awe and wonder and willingness fall to the background, and what rises is someone set in his/her ways. Someone you don't want to be. As I write this, the most common regrets people have in their lives include:

*I wish I hadn't worked so hard.*

*I should have stayed in touch with my friends.*

*I wish I had the courage to express my true self.*

*I wish I had let myself be happier.*

*I wish I led a life true to my dreams instead of what others expected of me.*

Those are incredibly powerful statements that all have a common thread—a lack of freedom in thoughts, emotions, and influences. The potential that lies in you and me is immense, yet it goes unfulfilled all too often. Courage and happiness seem to be in short supply and expectations are higher than they have ever been. Just as depression and substance abuse have increased and life expectancy rates have declined, the need for righteous oaks of strength and substance could not be greater than now!

- To call forward for courage that leads to happiness and purposeful satisfaction on a global scale is paramount.

- To plant acorns inspired by the Lord so that sturdy and righteous oak trees of men grow.

- To move toward integration of your mind, body, and soul instead of compartmentalizing and protecting those spaces that keep you from true freedom is key.

- To generate forces of strength and substance and pay it forward.

If you allow yourself to experience the richness and depth of becoming a source for others, you experience Kafele. As the source of life, the humility and fierceness you can discover in yourself will spread the acorns that Galatians 5:22 delivers:

> *But the fruit of the Spirit is of love, joy, peace, patience, kindness, goodness, faithfulness, gentleness, and self-control.*

Your authority will become authentic, your presence will reach far and wide and you will be sturdy like an oak tree on display for His splendor.

—BRITT

# About Britt Gusmus

Evolution … it's what you and I are meant to be … to do. From that football and baseball star in my youth; drafted to a professional team; to a star salesman; to a devoted family man. I began to ask: *What's next for me?*

The answers came … my next step ties to sharing what I've learned over four decades. The pathways that found my strength, developed my substance, and discovered my purpose. When spending time with a close friend in New Orleans, the power of *The Oak Tree Source* began to flow.

I no longer have the agility of that star quarterback or home run hitter, nor do I want to be a super building materials salesman. What I do want is to continue to be the husband and father I am … and continue improving in those roles. What I do want is to continue to work with and inspire youth in their aspirations through sports. And what I do want is to build a meaningful community for men to connect on deeper levels with their spirituality and purpose.

So … my question becomes:

What's next for you? Where do you want to evolve to?

## My Community

My community has been built and continues to be built upon a mutual drive and passion to see others live with purpose and share their stories of strength and substance. As an influencer and author, I aim to provide value to communities, schools, and organizations through experience, expertise, and motivation.

## Join My Journey

I am incredibly excited for the world to read my book, *The Oak Tree Source,* coming out in April 2022. Also, the Amazon best seller *The Impact of Influence* can be purchased on my website and on Amazon.

I can be found on:

Twitter@BrittGusmus

Instagram: BrittGusmus711

Facebook: Britt.Gusmus

Website: https://BrittGusmus.com/

Email: Britt@BrittGusmus.com

Each week I publish two video blogs: *Fired Up Friday* and *Sunday Encouragement.* Please tune in!

# Acknowledgments

*To my mom, Tricia Kruthaupt.* Your love, support, and enthusiasm for me cannot be measured by words alone. The stories are not always easy to revisit, but they made me who I am today and strengthened our relationship. I am incredibly grateful for all that you have done. There is more life to live! I love you!

*To my dad, Larry Gusmus.* I am blessed to have the good fortune to pick up your passion for life and charisma. I know you always had what was best for me in mind, I grateful for all of the ups and downs. I love you!

*To my brother, Benjamin.* I don't know what I would've have done without you. It brings me great joy to be your brother. We have so many great memories. Our relationship means more to me than you know. I admire the man you have become. I love you!

*To my LOMLW, Carrie.* You are a gift from God! I was never going to settle for a partner that was less than God's best for me. You are that blessing. I am so proud to walk this life shoulder to shoulder with you and love you the way you deserve. Thank you for choosing me. I love you with all that I've got. Our best is yet to come!

*To my daughter, Isabel.* Sweet, you are the realization of the dreams you mom and I had for building a family. I shake my head in awe and wonder of who you are and how much I love you! Each day I get to see you first thing in the morning fills my spirit with joy. I am so excited to see you continue to become an impactful young woman.

*To my son, Colt the Bolt.* You completed the Gusmus team! I am so blessed by your spirit, your imagination, and the possibilities you see. You make me so proud to be you father. I am so excited to support you in whatever you choose to pursue as you become strong and sturdy like an oak tree!

*To my Dragon's Den Softball Family.* You helped a broken boy become a man! Our friendships are so special to me. I love you guys!

*To my friends that I've known for over three decades.* You guys have seen me at my worst and my best. I love y'all! Thanks for always standing by me through it all.

*To my man, John Brooks.* Your friendship has shown me what it means to be an Oak Tree Source. I am forever grateful brother!

*To Judith Briles.* Thank you for helping make this story come to life. Your dedication and expertise making the *Oak Tree Source* the best it can be have been an incredible blessing! Thank you!

# How to Work with Britt

Bring Britt to your next conference, organizational event, or school.

As a sports coach and evangelist, he knows how to engage his participants from the moment his first sentence rolls out to create a transformative experience of inspiration and motivation. Britt knows how to inspire his audiences to action. And he knows how to deliver results.

Britt's audience favorites include:

*How to Become an Oak Tree Source*

*Creating an Inspired Connection*

*Growing in Intimacy with God*

*Mentoring the Acorns in Your Life*

*Creating the Acorn Factor*

*The Impact of Your Influence*

# How to Contact Britt

Call or email Britt for availability:

(720) 297-8067

Britt@BrittGusmus.com